Tent City Urbanism

From Self-Organized Camps to Tiny House Villages

Andrew Heben

Tent City Urbanism

From Self-Organized Camps to Tiny House Villages

Cover photograph (top) by author

Cover illustration (bottom) by Mark Lakeman

All interior photographs and graphics by author unless otherwise noted.

ISBN-13: 978-0692248058

Library of Congress Control Number: 2014944746

Discounts are available for ordering multiple copies so that you can share these ideas with friends, colleagues, or public officials to help start a village in your area. Please see the Village Collaborative website for details.

the **ViLLAGE COLLABORATiVE**

Eugene, Oregon | www.thevillagecollaborative.net

CONTENTS

PART IV | GUIDE

"Until the lions have their own historians,
the history of the hunt will always glorify the hunter."

— African Proverb

"There is no logic that can be superimposed on the city; people
make it, and it is to them, not buildings, that we must fit our plans."

— Jane Jacobs

Acknowledgments

Writing this book has led me to some of the most genuine, passionate, and dedicated people that I know. Meeting the people behind the various projects included here provided invaluable knowledge and inspiration, and this work would not be possible without the relationships developed along the way. In particular, I want to thank the following people:

My parents, Rick and Marcia, who provided me with the privilege of observing this topic from the position that I do. Charles Ellison, my thesis advisor at the University of Cincinnati, who first encouraged me to pursue this topic despite having little to go on at the time. Caleb Poirier, who invited me to come and stay at Camp Take Notice, and the others there that generously welcomed me into their community—a life altering experience that first inspired the writing of this book. Mark Lakeman, who showed me the true potential of a village and prompted my move to Oregon, which made all that unfolded afterwards possible. All those who have made Opportunity Village Eugene happen—especially our dedicated board of directors and volunteers, and the first members of Opportunity Village who have made it a success. My regular conversations with Jeff Albanese that challenged the ideas presented here to evolve for the better. Tom Atlee, whose editing, experience, and words of encouragement helped me pull it all together. And of course my partner, Joline Kessler, who joined me on many of the adventures included in this book and consistently supported its production.

Introduction

• • •

The Problem

Sprawling shantytowns may be a reality of Third World countries, but certainly not in the United States—right? To uphold this notion, we have adopted legal frameworks that make these informal settlements unlawful through various zoning, trespassing, and anti-camping regulations. Instead, one must purchase the right to land on which shelter is constructed, and even then, one must hire professionals to design and build the house, and apply for permits to certify that the shelter adheres to a standardized building code. A glaring problem with this approach is that not all citizens can or ever will meet the formal expectations of renting or owning a home. With the economic recession in 2008 followed by the housing foreclosure crisis in 2010, this truth has been brought to light for an even broader range of people.

While laws, property rights, and the specialization of home building give order to our society, they also ensure perpetual disorder and unrest through the creation of homelessness. This conflict has been exacerbated in recent years as greater demands are being placed on cities without the budgets to match. In 2013, a majority of states were still witnessing an increase in homelessness—even as federally mandated

10-year plans to "end homelessness" expired.¹ Meanwhile, in a survey by the U.S. Conference of Mayors, a majority of local leaders are expecting resources for providing emergency shelter to shrink.²

More so than ever we are finding ourselves in an all or nothing society. Historically, an abundance of single-room occupancy (SRO) hotels provided low-cost, short-term options in the private sector to fill this gap. From boarding and rooming houses to lodging and flophouses, affordable rooms could be rented by the day, week, or month at variable costs based on accommodations. But today they have become an endangered species.

Throughout the 20th century, minimum building standards were added that made the construction of new SROs unprofitable. And by the 1960s, existing buildings were closed and demolished throughout the country under the mask of "urban renewal." Since then, urban policies have largely held the development of low-income housing to middle-class standards. This has both improved the conditions of the bottom-rung of the housing market and eased neighboring concerns around adjacent property value. But at the same time, it has left the development of low-income housing inherently dependent upon government subsidies to be economically viable—subsidies that are consistently underfunded and in short supply.

With diminishing housing options, the gap between the "housed" and the "unhoused" has continued to swell, making it substantially more difficult for one to transition back into housing after losing it. Nowadays, if you are unable to secure government subsidized housing, you must come up with first and last months' rent or you are left with nothing. To be considered "affordable," housing is supposed to take up no more than 30 percent of your income, yet half of all renters are now paying a higher percentage (up from just over one-third in 2000). This has created what U.S. Housing Secretary Shaun Donovan has called, "the worst rental affordability crisis this country has ever known."³

By failing to provide adequate housing options while upholding the law, we have in fact erased the spaces in which many must live. Municipal and charitable homeless shelters are the last remaining safety net, yet these provisions have proven broadly insufficient, ineffective, and often inhumane.

Unsatisfied by the private, public, and non-profit sectors, the unhoused have taken to devising and implementing their own informal solutions. Some have opted to take this on alone, wandering the public realm during the day and finding a remote doorway come night. Others—often driven by a desire for stability, security, autonomy, and privacy—have found an alternative by banding together to form encampments. While some camps remain with only a few tight-knit members, others proliferate over time into what is commonly referred to as a "tent city."

Though far more stable than life on the street, members of the American tent city must still live with the constant uncertainty of whether or not their home will be there the next day. Local authorities will often dismantle these camps with little or no notice. In 2007—on the brink of a national economic recession—one of the more graphic examples occurred in St. Petersburg, Florida when police arrived at a self-organized tent city, slashed the tents with box cutter knives, and proceeded to dispose of the meager shelters and possessions within them as garbage.[4]

The Experience

In 2009, I began reading news articles telling of the rise of tent cities throughout the country, but they were largely signs of the times pieces without much substance. The subject would become the focus of my urban planning thesis project at the University of Cincinnati. So in the summer of 2010, I set out to visit a handful of the places that I had been reading about to see what I could uncover.

Packing our camping gear into the car, my partner and I headed north from Cincinnati to Ann Arbor where I had read of an established camp that was sticking together despite multiple evictions. From there we headed back south to Nashville where an unsanctioned tent city had existed in the same location since the 1980s. While a massive flood had left the makeshift settlement in ruins just a couple months prior to our trip, we decided to see what could still be uncovered there. Next, we stopped in Athens, Georgia where there had been reports of another venerable, informal tent city. And finally, we arrived in St. Petersburg, the site of the graphic tent slashing eviction from a few years back. There had been news of pushback as a result of the sweep-style tactics, and a sanctioned tent city had been established in unincorporated Pinellas County.

After this initial trip to gather research, I was most deeply impacted by my experiences in Ann Arbor, and so I returned for a month to live and participate in the unsanctioned tent city known as Camp Take Notice. The dedication to self-governance and the resulting sense of community is what attracted me to this camp in particular, but I was also inspired by the resilience of the group. Despite several attempts by local authorities to shut down their efforts, the tent city continued to relocate and stand together in solidarity.

At the time, this was an ideal focus for the thesis I had been piecing together—not only for the reasons stated above, but also because it currently existed at a legal crossroads. While the camp was still squatting on land illegally, they had been meeting regularly with public officials to discuss more formal solutions. By becoming an insider and gaining legitimacy within the camp, I found invaluable experiences that would become influential in the direction of my thesis—and in life in general.

Following graduation, I decided to take another road trip that next summer—this time an extended vacation rather than any intentional research. My partner and I headed west from Ohio, taking our time and camping in various national parks and forests along the way. We ended up in the Pacific Northwest, making our way to both Portland and Seattle. While we had wanted to visit this part of the country for other reasons, it happened to be home to the most noteworthy self-organized tent cities in the country. I had included them as case studies in my thesis project, but only based on what I had read from the limited resources available. Intrigued to learn more, I decided to make some more site visits.

While Couchsurfing in Portland we had a chance to stop in at Dignity Village—a permanent, sanctioned site where campers had moved out of tents and into more substantial micro-housing structures. Following the visit, I got a chance to sit down with Mark Lakeman, a visionary architect who assisted in the planning, design, and construction of the village. Heading north to Seattle, we made a stop at both Tent

City 3 and 4—itinerant, sanctioned camps that are required to pick-up and relocate every three months—along with a visit to the unsanctioned off-shoot, Nickelsville.

My thesis had focused primarily on the problem without getting too specific about any sort of solution. I had a lot of ideas about how things should be, but was only beginning to find the words to articulate them. But after my trip to the Northwest, many of the questions that arose from my experiences in Ann Arbor were beginning to find answers. I began to develop a more comprehensive vision for a "tent city urbanism"—a bottom-up approach to the provision of shelter based on observing and building upon existing patterns forged by the unhoused. Furthermore, it became increasingly clear that this topic had implications larger than just homelessness—it addressed our dire need for a cultural injection of community, democracy, and sustainability.

Shortly thereafter, I decided to make a move from Cincinnati to Portland since the city seemed to be a hospitable environment for the ideals that I wished to pursue. Lakeman, whom I met during my previous visit, provided me with a place to stay and became a mentor on this quest for truth and justice. However, my quixotic journey was soon cut short after taking a professional urban planning job two hours south in Eugene, Oregon.

While I was far from thrilled about moving away from Portland so quickly, it turned out to be an even riper environment. My arrival in Eugene coincided with the dismantling of the local Occupy camp, which had evolved from its original form as a place of protest to also encapsulate a place of refuge for more than 100 of the city's unsheltered population. The displacement of this mass of people catalyzed public concern around the issue of homelessness, leading to a mayor-appointed community task force responsible for finding "new and innovative solutions." From there, existing energy around the power of a self-organized camp converged with much of the research included in this book to create Opportunity Village—a self-governed community of thirty tiny houses for otherwise unhoused individuals and couples. The implementation of the project led to the formation of Opportunity Village Eugene, a non-profit organization that puts many of the ideas presented in this book into action locally.

The Book

The term "urbanism" commonly refers to the interaction between city dwellers and the built environment. A *tent city* urbanism, therefore, focuses on the character of tent cities, defined by the interaction between its members and the surrounding urban environment. Urbanism also implies a sense of progression—from early settlements to urban society. This book examines a microcosm of urbanization being carried out by the 21st century homeless and their advocates—progressing from tent to tiny house, from camp to village, and from emergency to transitional to affordable shelter.

These ad-hoc settlements take root in the cracks of the formal planning process. While they are often portrayed as a disorganized state of emergency, I find that the self-organized tent city actually addresses many of the shortfalls of more traditional responses to poverty. For example, they often exemplify self-management, direct democracy, tolerance, mutual aid, and resourceful strategies for living with less. Out of necessity, people have had to negotiate the sharing of space and resources, while unintentionally discovering the benefits of living in community.

Consequently, these tent cities provide a foundation for a village model—a model that physically builds upon the positive social elements of these camps by transitioning from tents to simple micro-housing structures, commonly known as tiny houses. This scenario improves the quality of life for the residents within, eases anxieties of the surrounding community, and sets a broader precedent for human-scale development with a light carbon footprint. Similar to the once popular SRO hotels, the village model provides a sense of ownership over a small, private space and combines that with shared, common spaces.

Tiny house villages offer a new paradigm for transitional and affordable housing that is more economically accessible and sustainable. The human-scale development can be carried out within a local community—establishing a grassroots model for developing low-cost housing without dependence on government subsidy. Additionally, it offers a more environmentally and socially sustainable housing option. Consequently, this book is intended not just for those looking for alternative solutions to homelessness, but also those seeking alternatives to conventional housing options. Alternatives that reduce human impact on our natural environment and focus on building communities rather than commodities. Unbeknownst to most, today's tent cities are opening the doors to sustainable development.

In Part I of the book, I further define a framework for progressing from tent cities to tiny house villages. Parts II and III then delve into case studies of a variety of camps and villages throughout the United States. While the examples may be well-known within their local communities, they are often treated as isolated occurrences. This book ties together these similar trends throughout the country to develop a more comprehensive vision. Based on firsthand experience, I describe how each provides a unique take on a common goal of developing a stable "place to be" for the unhoused.

Finally, Part IV provides a practical guide for catalyzing new and existing initiatives in other cities. The various case studies are synthesized to define an ecology of community-based models—including the Sanctuary Camp, the Rest Area, the Transitional Village, and the Affordable Village. Following this, I focus on putting ideas into action, with specific reference to my experience in advocating for, planning, designing, and building Opportunity Village.

Blurring the Line

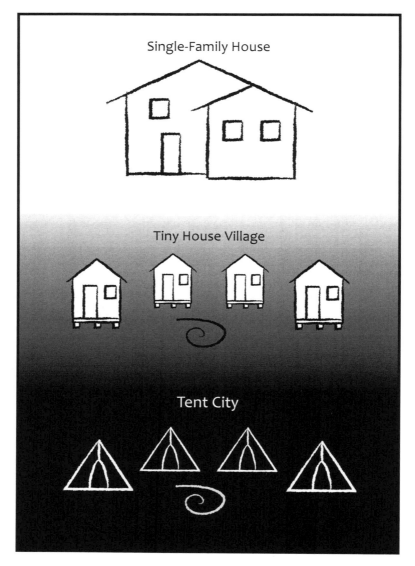

While some are upsizing from tent cities to tiny house villages, others are downsizing from conventional housing to similar tiny houses.

PART I | FRAMEWORK

PART I | FRAMEWORK

Chapter 1

Tent Cities Today

• • •

In February 2009, the American tent city suddenly took center stage following a special report on the *Oprah Winfrey Show*. Through the lens of a sprawling encampment along Sacramento's American River, the report aimed to "humanize" the economic recession. Tent cities were reported to be "makeshift shelters set up by people who have lost their homes and have nowhere to go." Each person who appeared on screen gave a heart-wrenching story of recently losing his or her job to the recession, followed by losing his or her home to foreclosure. The conditions in Sacramento were said to be just one example in the "explosion of tent cities across America."[5]

Concurrently, Justin Sullivan of Getty Images released a photo essay documenting the very same camp.[6] Existing conditions were juxtaposed with photographs of similar camps along the American River during the Great Depression—an unmistakable reference to the start of a Second Great Depression. These older camps of the 1930s were known as "Hoovervilles," named after president Herbert Hoover, who was commonly thought to have been responsible for the desperate conditions that led to the development of the sprawling shantytowns in cities throughout the country.

The photographs evoke sympathy by capturing the forlorn expressions of the victims with close-ups of the meager possessions that filled the camp. There is one, however, that stands out from the dismal tone set by the rest. Set in the depression days of 1936 Sacramento, it depicts a middle-aged man leaning back in his lawn chair with laundry hanging on a line in the background. He wears a wide smile as a small child and dog jump onto his lap while another young boy leans over the scene, also smiling. It reveals a rare glimpse into the lighter side of camp life, highlighting the resilience of humans to adapt when presented with challenges. Their possessions may be few but they will endure as a family.

Following this initial coverage, the tent city story was exhausted by news sources across the country. Headlines read "Slumdog USA" and "Cities Deal with Surge in Shantytowns." The stories described the conditions in Sacramento along with similar tent cities that seemed to have abruptly surfaced throughout the country as a result of economic disaster. Today's camps were satirically referred to as "Bushvilles" or "Obamavilles" depending upon the political affiliation of the source. Curious as to just how widespread this so-called phenomenon really was, I began tracking news stories on tent cities throughout the country, and quickly mapped dozens of cities with a local camp documented since 2009. The inventory that was compiled is in no way comprehensive, but alludes to the overall extent of these informal settlements.

Why were America's homeless suddenly receiving so much attention when the news media typically avoids intractable social issues at all costs? As one journalist put it, "The story is compelling precisely because it is so visual."[7] Homelessness is usually a piecemeal experience for the housed. Walking in an urban area, one is likely to pass someone holding a sign asking for money, pushing a shopping cart full of personal belongings, or sleeping in a doorway. These are frequent but isolated encounters. The number of people going unhoused may be large but they are dispersed, and the true scale of the issue is hidden. But with a photograph of a tent city, the housed can now place an image to the overwhelming numbers reported by regular point-in-time homeless counts. The experience is no longer isolated and the scale of the issue becomes unavoidably obvious. The same journalist expands on

Tent Cities Documented in the United States
(2009-2014)

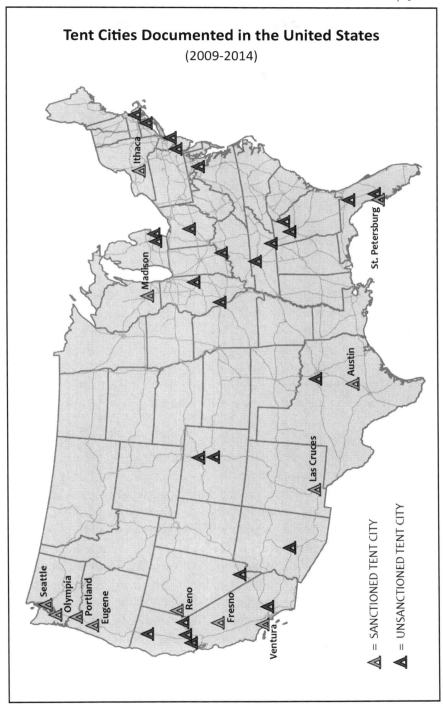

the appeal behind this story: "The poverty doesn't need to be explained. Instead it can be shown, along with a caption explaining that this is the new face of homelessness and poverty in post-boom, recession-era America. A gleaming city skyline as a backdrop to immiseration. Rio, or Mumbai, on the American River."[8]

The tent city story of 2009 went on to receive coverage from major international news sources like the *BBC* and *Al Jazeera*. These reports used the informal camps to illustrate just how bad conditions had gotten in the United States—the world's economic leader now has shantytowns! The UK's *Daily Mail* ran the headline "The credit crunch tent city which has returned to haunt America," which dramatically described the scene:

> A century and a half ago it was at the centre of the California gold rush, with hopeful prospectors pitching their tents along the banks of the American River. Today, tents are once again springing up in the city of Sacramento. But this time it is for people with no hope and no prospects. With America's economy in freefall and its housing market in crisis, California's state capital has become home to a tented city for the dispossessed... The tents and other makeshift homes have sprung up in the shadow of Sacramento's skyscrapers.[9]

While these stories may be eye-catching, they are remarkably superficial and lack any real substance other than highlighting the fact that people are, out of necessity, living in tents. The tent cities were ubiquitously portrayed as mere symbols of poverty—the physical manifestations of our nation's foreclosure crisis—with no attention given to the longevity, organization, or diversity of the camps. Instead, they imply disorder and strive to evoke awe, sympathy, and sometimes disgust. But did these informal settlements really just appear out of thin air following economic hardship? Even the homeless advocates interviewed in the stories seem to focus only on the tragedy of the situation—that the encampments are a testament to our failure to provide adequate affordable housing. Is there no positive side to people with no place else to go having a place to be? Fortunately, with time, more detailed information became available about today's tent cities.

A Better Perspective

By March 2010, the National Coalition for the Homeless released a special report—"Tent Cities in America"—that provided more detailed information on the so-called recent phenomenon. "Tent Cities are America's de facto waiting room for affordable and accessible housing," writes executive director, Neil Donovan. "The idea of someone living in a tent in this country says little about the decisions made by those who dwell within and so much more about our nation's inability to adequately respond to our fellow residents in need."[10] Similar to the media's perspective, advocates for the homeless continue to point to the camps as tragic symbols of just how bad conditions have gotten. Tent city is a state of emergency from which people must be rescued, but how and where to is left unclear.

Originally intending to provide national coverage through a series of regional reports, the West Coast was the only region that ended up being surveyed by the Coalition. This was an appropriate starting point since the region contained the most established camps in the country, some of which were among the first to be formalized and regulated. Tent cities are defined as "a variety of temporary housing facilities that often use tents." Though not terribly descriptive, it demonstrates a more investigative approach to the issue and implies an exploration of the various types of camps. The names and locations of select tent cities are listed along with key characteristics of each. "Encampments range in structure, size and formality," the document reports, "Larger more formal tent cities are often named and better known, but don't represent the majority of tent city structures or residents, found with smaller populations and dimensions."[11]

The report gathers ground level research in the field, providing a much-needed analytical perspective of the issue. It becomes evident that while our attention to tent cities may be related to economic conditions, their existence is not. They are in fact a deeply rooted trend in the American city. Examples such as Dignity Village in Portland and Tent City 3 in Seattle were both established in 2000, during times of economic prosperity. Furthermore, while the recent tent city in Sacramento was extensively compared to the Hooverville that existed there during the Great Depression, it is pointed out that camps have existed in some form or another in that area along the American River *since the 1930s*:

> The banks of the American and Sacramento Rivers in downtown Sacramento have long been a site for homeless encampments dating back to the Great Depression. There have been dozens of scattered campsites for decades along the rivers and in the areas close-by. Periodically law enforcement would dismantle the settlements and take the possessions of many of the homeless people, claiming that they had the legal right to confiscate property under the city's harsh anti-camping ordinance. After a federal civil rights lawsuit was brought against the city and county of Sacramento, an unannounced, informal moratorium on enforcement of the anti-camping camping ordinances ensued. This allowed the growth of "Tent City," with hundreds of campers congregated on one site because the city and county felt vulnerable to further costly litigation... The American River encampment had been a relatively small settlement until the unannounced moratorium on the anti-camping ban took effect after the lawsuit was filed against the city, at which point it quickly grew and stabilized with 100-250 campers at any given time.[12]

While it may be true that this was the largest camp the area had seen since the Hooverville days, the report highlights that the recent economic recession was not to blame for the size as much as the change in the enforcement of laws that make these living conditions illegal. In a survey of 97 Sacramento campers in March of 2009, 35 percent reported that they had become unhoused in the past year.[13] The proportion is certainly high, but it does not represent the majority of the population being served by the tent city. So, while the informal settlements may be influenced by economy, they are affected more so by policy.

Anti-camping ordinances are now commonplace in cities throughout the United States, but Sacramento is home to one of the strictest. The city prohibits camping on private property, even with permission, for longer than twenty-four hours. Relaxing the enforcement of this law is what allowed the camp to swell. The media frenzy only brought widespread attention to the camp after placing a global spotlight on it, leading embarrassed city officials to disband the camp shortly thereafter on grounds of unsafe and unsanitary conditions.

Breaking it Down

A tent city is a well-rooted homeless encampment, often with some level of organizational structure and an indefinite population. There is no set size at which an encampment becomes a tent city. Instead, it is an abstract label that is eventually adopted by its inhabitants and sometimes by the surrounding community—providing a sense of identity to an otherwise unrelated group of people experiencing homelessness.

Tent cities can be categorized into two main types based on legal status. Some are *sanctioned*, meaning they have been formalized and regulated by a municipality in some way or another. All others can be referred to as *unsanctioned*, meaning they exist illegally by squatting on public or private land. There are a variety of ways in which municipalities have gone about sanctioning a tent city—including conditional use permits, planned unit developments, zoning for camping, and emergency orders. While the "Tent Cities in America" report focuses on these sanctioned examples, comparatively they are rare and the majority of camps are unsanctioned and undocumented. The sanctioned examples are, however, leading a tent city movement that is offering innovative solutions to a situation that is largely regarded as intolerable or deviant.

The designation of sanctioned or unsanctioned status is not always obvious, though. Once discovered, many camps exist in a grey area where they are technically illegal, but there is no foreseeable action taken to evict them. This grey area is the result of the ethical dilemma presented by the issue, and the contentious nature of laws that make such simple acts like sleep illegal. While not sanctioning the tent city, some city leaders have unofficially agreed to not evict a specific camp—such as the case with Seattle's Nickelsville, which informally accommodated over 100 unhoused individuals, couples, and families. Others have enacted a moratorium on the camping ban—often as a result of lawsuits—that allow camps to informally expand like the example in Sacramento.

While these camps are still considered unsanctioned, they become significantly more stable, which leads to the next method for categoriz-ing tent cities—level of organization. Some are *self-organized*, developing some sense of order through democratic meetings and community agreements. Others are *unorganized*, consisting of people simply living next to each other out of necessity. Granted, there is always some level of organization in any human settlement, but these examples consist of a minimal amount. Similar to legal status, many exist somewhere in between these distinctions, demonstrating aspects of both ends of the spectrum.

In the process of sanctioning a tent city, there are diverse models that have emerged for doing so, often influenced by the amount and source of funding. All sanctioned examples are supported by a partner-ship with a non-profit organization, but the nature of this relationship varies widely. Some organizations support a *self-managed* model, leav-ing decision-making, operation, and maintenance in the hands of the residents themselves. These are typically citizen-driven initiatives that require minimal funding. Others adopt a more *charitable* model, organized similar to the traditional social service model where help is handed down from specialist to client. This is often the result of signifi-cant funding from governments or institutions.

Together, the variable dynamics of legal status, level of organiza-tion, and type of funding create a conceptual field on which each tent city can be placed. Where a particular tent city falls in this field often influences the permanence of the camp—certainly one of the most controversial points of discussion around this issue. Are they to be *tem-porary*, providing emergency shelter under special circumstance for a limited amount of time? Or are they more *permanent*, filling a gap in our existing housing system? If so, must they be *itinerant*, and required to move locations after a set duration of time? This is a complex dilemma that will be explored throughout this book.

In a paper focusing on the politics of tent cities, Katherine Long-ley discusses how the permanence of tent cities is always in question. She describes the space in which tent cities exist as a "constant battle-ground" where members of a tent city are striving for a "semblance of permanence from day to day" while the larger community is unwill-ing to recognize the tent as a "viable permanent dwelling" and instead sees the tent as a "symbol of poverty" that threatens the stability of the surrounding neighborhood.[14] She concludes that this is an unwinnable battle for both sides. While the larger community may succeed in evicting the tent city from a specific site, they will likely fail in removing it from the community altogether. Instead, the tent city will simply move to a new location.

Due to this conflict of interest, choice of location becomes a critical factor in determining the longevity of a tent city. Some are *hidden*, tucked into a defensible residual space. Forested left-over spaces carved by highways or rivers are often ideal locations for this. Others are more *visible*, existing within the public's view. These examples are often quickly dismantled unless they can be positioned as a protest with adequate political support. As a result, most unsanctioned camps take to hiding to establish a better sense of stability. If a visible location is sought out, it is typically either an attempt to make a statement or a sign of more lenient law enforcement. Sanctioned tent cities present a similar trend. If a marginalized location is established at the *edge* of the city, far away from residential zones, the permanence of the community is less likely to be in question than if it takes a *central* location within the urban core. As a result, a legal place of refuge is often established at the expense of further alienating the population from the rest of the city.

A View of Camp Life

My initial trip to spend time at tent cities in Ann Arbor, Nashville, Athens, and St. Petersburg provided me with a more intimate understanding of these informal settlements. Each stop was distinct from the next. Reflecting on the various dynamics of each, I found that a tent city is not only defined by the criteria previously listed—it is also a unique product of its local context. Geographic climate, style of local governance, attitude of the surrounding community, availability of services, and the intentions and personalities of its members are all critical characteristics that shape the organization of a tent city.

For example, a different approach must be taken during the harsh winters in Ann Arbor—where camp populations drop as emergency shelters open—when compared to St. Petersburg, which sees an influx of unhoused individuals migrate from the north to avoid cold weather. Also of note, the first tent cities to be sanctioned are all found along the West Coast, where the political climate is typically considered to be more progressive than other parts of the country. The attitude a city takes towards its homeless population dramatically influences where a tent city will locate, how long it can exist before being dismantled, and the potential for developing a legal solution.

Most importantly, tent cities are a reflection of the people who compose them. The personalities and intentions of the people in the camp seems to be the most critical factor in shaping the level of organization that exists within the community. Are they interested in making a statement or simply trying to get by? Do they want to improve their situation, have they given up hope, or are they just looking for an alternative to the demands of traditional housing? These initial site visits left me with a better understanding of this population, which has been influential in guiding the findings and vision presented in this book.

While talking with members of the various tent cities, I asked them to rank the type of shelter they would most prefer. Nearly everyone responded affordable housing as a first choice, followed by a tent city as a second alternative. The third choice was mixed—some preferred the local shelter while others preferred the street. This illustrates the critical view of the traditional, charitable shelter system held by the homeless. Not only did the majority of people prefer a tent city even if there was space available in the shelter, but several would choose life on the street over the shelter as well. The preference of the tent city was largely attributed to the sense of autonomy and safety that the informal communities offer.

A few individuals even preferred the tent city to affordable housing, which demonstrates that some will always prefer to remain outside of conventional housing. I found that a large sector of this population was veterans who had become accustomed to the camaraderie and rugged, do-it-yourself lifestyle that comes with military training and combat. Others were simply bohemians dedicated to an alternative, "off-the-grid" way of life. As described in *The Last Great American Hobo*, this is a preference for the concrete over the abstract —a choice to confront the "two lions" of food and shelter, which are each "a definite enemy, a certain nightmare," rather than facing the "ever marching hoard of rats" that come with a conventional lifestyle, and are sure to consume you in the end no matter how hard you try.[15]

However, the majority of tent city inhabitants portrayed a strong sense of shame when questioned about their living situation. This seemed to result from the expected necessity of an expression of urgency and desperation from a person in their situation. However, the longer I stayed at Camp Take Notice, the more I came to question the authenticity of these initial responses. There seemed to be a certain degree of contentment with life in a tent city, but one that could never be fully disclosed in a casual encounter or interview out of fear of being stigmatized as lazy. Along with the high regard for individual autonomy, I believe this sense of contentment to be a result of the "community feel" found in the informal living situation. I hesitate to lean on that phrase, which is so often abused by politicians and planners, but it seems that these places are at the heart of what the phrase "community feel" is attempting to convey. Rather than dismissing the American tent city as a mere symbol of our nations economic hardship, just maybe it is alluding to a more sustainable and fulfilling housing option—socially, economically, and environmentally.

Chapter 2

Controlling & Reclaiming Space

• • •

The right to space in the city is ever-changing with the tides of con-trol and resistance. This creates transitional spaces, where the physical space in question is constantly being claimed and shaped by oppos-ing forces. The unhoused—those without the right to a space of their own—must live their entire lives within the public realm, and so there is little distinction between public and private. Cities often confront this uncomfortable reality through the use of environmental design that alters public space to be unaccommodating to those who must live there. Classic examples in public parks include designing benches so that people cannot lie down and special trash cans that restrict glean-ing cans and bottles. Downtown exclusion zones go further to prohibit specific activities—often geared toward those not participating in com-merce—and ban those with citations from the defined area.

Residual public spaces are defended through other tactics. Some cities have taken to cutting down trees around highway interchanges to expose unwanted inhabitants, and landscaping with large rocks under bridges to eliminate the possibility. Even the selection of certain plant species can be employed to prevent people from sleeping in hidden areas between the plantings and a building.

As a result, the unhoused are often left to develop alternative and innovative techniques for resisting these measures of control. The self-organized tent city is a physical embodiment of this resistance, where the unhoused are reclaiming a space of their own within a community. The American tent city, therefore, is a non-violent revolution that directly responds to the absence of place and participation in today's city. Just as formal actors are trying to control space, those with no place else to go are reclaiming it. As part of their resistance, the unhoused claim autonomy for their cultural and physical place and continually remake it to fit their needs—just as the formal actors continually tear it down to remake it according to their own designs.

Looking at the post-modern American city, we see a persistent homeless population, tightening budgets, and the damaging effects of some people not having a stable space to call home. We see the need for some kind of security in place, a sense of place, of purpose, and of belonging. At the same time we see vacant and underutilized land, an excess of materials going unused, and lots of people who want and need something meaningful to do. It seems only logical then to better utilize the resources available within our local communities to develop sensible, low-cost solutions.

Instead, we rely almost exclusively on federal and state funding to pay service providers that hand help down. The familiar goal to "end homelessness"—both locally and nationally—is almost always sought through plans that attempt to modify people in order to fit a narrow conception of space. Thought is rarely given to the other side of the spectrum—altering our ideas of urban space to fit the needs of people.

Rather than continuing to seek eviction, I argue that we should be looking to accommodate these alternative forms of emergency shelter to develop a form of transitional and affordable housing suitable to this population. Currently, there is a clear dichotomy between the formal city solution and the informal human solution. We need cities with formal human solutions. The task requires collaboration and careful compromise to develop a solution that works for all parties involved, and some of the examples in this book show how this is possible. The result is a city with a greater sense of social inclusion, which can be beneficial to everyone.

The Grid City

Our understanding of space has been heavily influenced by the grid plan that defines the layout of the American city. Mark Lakeman, co-founder of Portland's City Repair project, often points to this as the root cause of the prevalent social isolation that has left much of today's cities in disrepair. The grid plan was first developed between 3,000 BC and 200 BC in the Euphrates Valley, originating as a military camp plan devised as a means to divide and conquer. It has since become well respected as an efficient and convenient form of city planning. While most U.S. cities are now designed around the grid, few recognize that this was not by democratic choice but by mandate.[16]

The earliest New England colonies had concentric layouts, radiating out from a central meeting house and town square, and the grid was largely unknown to these modest, self-managed villages. The settlements were also geomorphic in that they adapted to the context established by natural features. The communities were self-contained, both economically and culturally, and so did not accommodate continual growth and expansion. But with the transition from the colonial village to the commercial town at the end of the 17th century, "The common concerns of all the townsfolk took second rank: the privileges of the great landlords and merchants warped the development of the community."[17]

With the enactment of the National Land Ordinance of 1785, the remaining frontier was divided into a continental grid, and all towns and cities established thereafter were required to be developed using a grid plan. However, Lakeman emphasizes that the ordinance lacks any mandate for public squares, and notes that the absence of these places combined with the grid plan had austere consequences on the cities established during westward expansion:

> Only a decade after the public spaces of the commons had been so crucial to the American Revolution, how could the Continental Congress have forgotten such an evidently vital provision as public gathering places? By this omission, the grid of the urban realm in America is reduced virtually to its original form in Assyria. Mitigated by many political freedoms, the provision of parks, the in-

spiring presence of a dynamic, open landscape, and a recent history of social and economic improvements through struggle, the American grid nonetheless remains a powerful geometry of isolation which encourages conformity and disassociation... The placeless geometry of the grid, which serves to defeat localized social identity and eliminate local community space, always establishes a standardized landscape designed to engender a homogenizing effect on its inhabitants.[18]

Power and control is embedded in the very core of our urban design, which has had significant implications on the way we think—or maybe more appropriately, don't think—about the use of physical space. The grid largely ignores social and natural concerns, and instead reinforces political and economic structures based upon competition and expansion above all else.

The consequences are particularly harsh for those left without a right to a piece of the grid, which purposefully keeps property and economic freedom out of common reach. Where are they supposed to go? Naturally, this population has historically established off-the-grid alternatives to simply get by from day-to-day, as exemplified by the self-organized tent cities covered in this book. However, over the course of the past century, policies have been put in place to further tighten the control of our physical environment. What has ensued is similar to the once popular "whack-a-mole" arcade game. Just as policymakers cover one hole in the grid, the same issue persistently pops out of a new one.

The Demise of Low-Cost Housing

In the past, the grid city was also mitigated by a diversity of low-cost housing options in the private market. An abundance of single room occupancy (SRO) hotels flourished in U.S. cities of the early 20th century, ranging from rooming houses for the middle class to lodging houses for the lower class. Just within lodging houses, accommodations ranged from private rooms (dorms) to large rooms broken into cubicles (cages) to bunk rooms with rows of beds to a few square feet of space on a floor (flops)—with each getting progressively cheaper. As a result the homeless and nearly homeless had a variety of alternative forms of shelter to choose from, which has been well described by Hoch and Smith:

> In many cases the choice was made for the individual, in a sense, by economic conditions. Housing was a fluid and uncertain situation; eventually most of the population used all the alternatives—cages, flops, dorms, and the streets—at one time or another. When this law did not apply, when a very minimal amount of discretionary income was available, the hobo or tramp or bum was a fee agent. And whenever this was the case, the housing of choice was the cage hotel... The reason for the success of the cage hotels, aside from the fact they filled the desperate need for housing, was that they provided other advantages: privacy and freedom. Every room had its own lock and key, and the resident could come and go as he pleased... The popularity of cage hotels did not stem from any great improvement in the physical setting (which was marginal at best), but rather in the qualitative benefits of a private room.[19]

Essentially, classic SRO housing consisted of very small private spaces—which itself varied significantly based upon price—along with common facilities that usually included a bathroom down the hall and a shared kitchen and dining room on a separate floor. The dense housing was also supported by mixed-use neighborhoods where surrounding stores and public spaces became extensions of each resident's home. This arrangement was valued not because it met certain material standards, but because it was economical yet still respected an individual's privacy and autonomy.

It is important to note that the availability of this housing option did not necessarily result in a concentration of those on the bottom rung of society. The arrangement also appealed to a healthy mix of the middle class—including young adults looking to start a career, artists, students, and blue-collar workers. It was not until suburbanization, the accompanying ethos of individualism, and eventually the deinstitutionalization of mental health facilities that led to a homogenized population of tenants who were down-and-out. In addition, SROs were crippled by urban policies intended to eliminate traditional low-income housing, a changing economy with diminishing demand for transient labor and higher rates of unemployment, and welfare plans that undermined the autonomy of the poor.[20]

The vibrant, walkable neighborhoods decayed as urban areas experienced widespread disinvestment. Attention was instead turned to auto-oriented development just outside the city. And by 1950, more people would live in suburbs than in cities. Many jobs were still downtown, but highways, parking garages, and skyways allowed for a commute without ever stepping foot on a sidewalk. Beginning with the "urban renewal" programs of the 1960s, neighborhoods identified as a blight were completely razed—often as a result of conveniently routed highway construction. The existing SRO districts were depleted, and often replaced with a smaller quantity of single-use apartment buildings.

Furthermore, zoning and building code provisions had been put in place to ensure the demise of SRO type housing. Zoning was used to corner the use in the oldest parts of town, and changes to the building code made it difficult, if not impossible, to build new SRO housing. The first step was to limit the minimum square footage for a habitable space, followed by requiring each unit to have its own bathroom and kitchen. This significantly drove the cost of development up, making it economically unviable to build very low-income housing on the private market. Off-street parking requirements, which now usually require at least one space per unit, have added an even more insuperable burden.[21]

While housing reformers—both well-intended and self-seeking— celebrated improvements in the minimum standard of living, the act removed the bottom-end of private housing from the market by making it too expensive to develop and manage. This has led to the current dilemma where, in order to be affordable to low-income tenants, housing is inherently dependent on government subsidies that have been made to be in short supply. Today, the construction of low-income housing comes at a cost of upwards of $200,000 per unit—similar to the average sales price of a single-family house in many areas.

In his short e-book on this subject, Alan Durning argues that it is once again time to allow the generation of inexpensive, housing options to supplement the shortfall of public subsidies. And, he points out a way for doing so that, while vehemently guarded, is not as complex as we might think—we just need to do away with regulations that simply protect adjacent property values by defining "decent housing" based on middle-class expectations.[22]

The situation highlights the influence of the grid, which reinforces attention to property value where the house is a commodity to be bought and sold. This has created an inflated standard of living where middle-class values determine what is and isn't acceptable—even when some are content with less. While limiting profit-hungry landlords from taking advantage of tenants is a legitimate concern, minimum square footage, kitchen, bathroom, and parking requirements go beyond the building codes foremost focus of life safety provisions and structural collapse. Instead, under the shroud of health and welfare, the code has come to mandate middle-class norms and eliminate simpler housing options that are perceived to negatively influence adjacent property value. But by failing to ensure that everyone can meet those standards, we have in fact jeopardized the life safety of an entire segment of the population.

Broken Windows in the New Urban Frontier

By the 1980s, space in some city centers began to receive a renewed sense of value. Urban areas became a new "wild west" for artists followed by young professionals, creating what Neil Smith called "the new urban frontier."[23] By the time development had finally sprawled as far as it could functionally reach from the city, the urban center once again became a place to explore and tame. This meant that the cost of renting the most affordable apartments went up, and neighborhoods were gentrified as existing tenants were pushed out. With a renewed interest in urban living, many cities are now reinvesting in what's left of their deteriorating SRO housing stock. However, they are being reincarnated as boutique hotels to spur economic development rather than provide low-income housing.[24]

The Lower East Side of New York City provides an early example of this national phenomenon as described by Smith. After widespread gentrification of the neighborhood resulted in the infamous 1988 riot at Tompkins Square Park, a few dozen unhoused people began to use the public space as a new home. Many had recently lost their housing nearby but refused to leave the neighborhood, and one resident described it as "the place for one last metaphorical stand" against gentrification. By 1991, there were around one hundred shanties and tents occupying the park when the police evicted over 300 people and quickly barricaded the site with a fence. After closing the park, several smaller tent cities formed in adjacent vacant lots, only to soon be bulldozed and also fenced. Finally, the economic refugees were routed underneath nearby bridges or any available space concealed from public view.[25]

The taming of this new urban frontier, among other things, meant clearing the unhoused from sight. As cities became fixed on measures of "livability" in an effort to attract capital, local governments began to practice "the annihilation of space by law"—using legal remedies to physically erase the spaces in which the unhoused must live.[26]

Kelling and Wilson justified this initiative in 1982 with their "broken windows" theory, which offered a new approach for policing urban areas. The theory asserts that a broken window in a city implies that "no one cares," and will inevitably lead to more broken windows. An experiment of two untended cars—one in the Bronx and one in Palo Alto—was used to test the theory. Both cars were eventually heavily vandalized, though the more prominent location in Palo Alto needed a little kick-start before the defacement ensued. From here, Kelling and Wilson make the conclusion that social ills that are visible in a city will inevitably lead to more, and likely worse, social decay. They assert, "the unchecked panhandler is in fact the first broken window."[27] In other words, broken people in public spaces results in more broken people.

The theory suggests a strict enforcement of "quality of life crimes" such as panhandling, loitering, and public intoxication or urination—with the idea that these acts infringe on the quality of life for others in the city. The phrase is quite ironic since many of these crimes are actually a consequence of the quality of life of the offender. In the past, these minor acts had been commonly overlooked in urban areas in order to concentrate policing efforts on more severe crimes. However, the broken windows theory asserts that it is in fact these minor crimes that lead criminals to believe they can get away with much more serious crimes like rape, murder, and theft. So by eliminating petty crimes, a city could in turn prevent more violent crimes. The widespread acceptance of this premise marks a drastic shift from "servicing" toward "policing" as a method for managing the issue of homelessness.

With the rise of Mayor Rudolph Giuliani in 1994, New York City became the first city to fully adopt the broken windows theory. The so-called quality of life crimes were enforced more strictly than ever, and the unhoused were either arrested or told to move along. Giuliani proclaimed, "You are not allowed to live on a street in a civilized city. It is not good for you; it is not good for us. Maybe the city was stupid enough to embrace that idea years ago. We care about you enough and are not that dumb to think you should live on streets. So we contact and tell you, you have got to move."[28] As is common, the only problem with the mayor's benevolence was that he did not provide a viable alternative to those living on the street. In fact, his first budget proposed that the homeless pay rent for nights spent in city run shelters.

New York City's focus on petty crimes did see promising results. Crime rates dropped, and in 2002 Manhattan had the lowest murder rate it had seen in a century. The number of homicides in 2000 dropped 73 percent when compared to 1990.[29] But did citing panhandlers really deter murder? It is not evident how much the enforcement of quality of life crimes contributed to the shift. Experts have offered everything from economic prosperity to legalized abortion as a reason for the significant reduction in crime. Levitt and Dubner argue that removing "broken windows" actually had little effect at all. They cite two reasons to support this claim. First, the homicide rate had already dropped 20 percent before Giuliani was elected—meaning the shift was well under way prior to the new policing strategies being adopted. Second, the New York Police Department was expanded by 45 percent between 1991 and 2001—over three times the national average during this period.[30] A more logical reason for the reduction in crime, then, may have been the drastic increase in police force, not necessarily the change in strategy. Regardless, after New York City's success, cities across the country began to institute the broken windows theory, cracking down on quality of life crimes.

While conversations around policing the homeless are often varied and distorted by political ideology, evaluating the practice from an economic perspective is difficult to dispute. What is the cost of controlling space? While some may agree with these policies, do they want to personally pay for it with their tax dollars? A study comparing nine major U.S. cities found that incarceration and hospitalization are far more expensive routes than providing shelters or even supportive housing. Of the nine cities surveyed, the average cost per day for each setting was: Hospital, $1,638; Mental Hospital, $550; Jail, $81; Prison, $79; Supportive housing, $30; Shelter, $28.[31] Simply providing a legal "place to be" would therefore benefit both the unhoused and the fiscal conservative. A recent study in Central Florida quantifies this economic benefit—showing that the public expenses that are incurred by leaving someone on the street comes at an annual cost of $31,065 per person. Meanwhile, providing that person with permanent housing, job training, and health care was found to cost taxpayers 68 percent less at $10,051.[32] The alternative models for emergency, transitional, and affordable shelter that are documented in this book have proven to be an even more cost-effective measure. This is made possible by retaining one distinguishing characteristic: self-management.

Reclaiming Democracy

While the conflict has been presented as a battle for space, it is usually a rather one-sided fight with formal actors wielding all the power, and the informal actors doing the best they can to stay out of sight. But in the past, the tent cities and shantytowns of America have located in more public spaces. For example, during the early 1930s, there was an infamous "Hooverville" located on what is now the Grand Lawn of New York City's Central Park. Recognizing the severity of the economic situation and the widespread unemployment of the time, it was recorded that the public and political sentiment was largely *with* the shantytowns. Contrary to today's coverage, they were described as symbols of "ingenuity." In 1932, *The New York Times* reported that the city's Park Department halfheartedly intended to bulldoze the shantytown. "We don't want to do it but we can't help it," said the Deputy Parks Commissioner, adding, "although the men had maintained good order, had built comfortable shacks and furnished them as commodiously as they could, there were no water or sanitary facilities near the settlement."[33] The Tompkins Square Park camp described earlier is another very public example that was around for years in the 1980s. However, following the adoption of the broken windows theory, visible public space ceased to be a viable option for most.

In their article "Reclaiming Space," Groth and Corijn advocate for informal actors—such as the members of tent cities—to take a stronger role in setting the urban agenda. They begin with the assertion that post-modern planning has failed to respond to post-modern urbanism. Comparatively, the modern city consisted of a homogenized population with a clear agenda, and centralized planning agencies were able to use order and rationality to serve this relatively uniform society. The result was what Jane Jacobs described in 1961 as "a city of monotony, sterility, and vulgarity."[34]

On the contrary, the post-modern city has witnessed the emergence of a more pluralistic society with highly differentiated agendas. As a result, post-modernist planning theory has attempted to become more flexible, but Groth and Corijn argue that planners still encourage spaces "catered for a relatively uniform society in a system of mass production and mass consumption."[35] Formal strategies limit the complexity of the city and aim to establish a predictable population. This diminishes the "dimension of socioeconomic richness and cultural mobility upon which the traditional metropolis thrives," and instead we are left with a streamlined city, where "staged images of the public replace the spaces of idiosyncratic interaction."[36]

"Reclaiming Space" calls for an alternative approach in which urban spatial structures diverge from "active repossessions" and "symbolic reconstructions" to create a city with a greater sense of social inclusion. Residual space, which lacks any significant economic value, is identified as a suitable place for this type of urban transformation to occur. Here, Groth and Corijn argue that formal planning and politics should step aside to allow space for more informal development.

Today's tent cities organized by the unhoused offer a prime example of this type of reclamation of space. Due to the negligence of formal actors, marginalized members of the city are taking matters into their own hands. Out of necessity, they are rediscovering the power of community, and through this collective effort, people in a similar situation are forging their own solutions by claiming space and working together to improve their individual situations. Rather than settling in popular public spaces, these economic refugees tend to seek hidden residual spaces where they are far less likely to be bothered. Camps tend to most often form in the left-over spaces carved by highways, railroads, or rivers. The latter has proven problematic for many cities, with the unhoused locating in environmentally sensitive areas like wetlands and floodplains since these are often large tracts of land isolated from the public. While they are out of sight, the lack of infrastructure can lead to the degradation of these protected ecological areas. This is probably the most reasonable justification for evicting a camp—and tends to receive public support from both the right and left—but it is typically out of a lack of options that these sites are chosen. This makes an environmental case for establishing a legal "place to be" on a site that is appropriate for human habitation.

But the endorsement of the broken windows theory suggests that these informal settlements are robbing a certain degree of quality of life from the surrounding, housed community. Furthermore, the settlements thwart the efforts by formal design to establish predictable behavior. As a result, laws and strategies have been adopted to disrupt these acts of necessity, exiling those without a right to space in the city to an itinerant lifestyle.

However, the kind of informal tent community that I am describing actually returns some quality of life to the population within, and by applying the same logic behind the broken windows theory positively, this benefits the surrounding population as well. Simply allowing for a legal place to reside—even with the most meager provisions of shelter—reduces negative, external impacts on the city. In fact, one could argue that these people are no longer homeless. I mentioned this notion to several people living at Camp Take Notice, and each considered his or her simple tent to be a home for the time being, even though it may not conform to conventional standards of a house. This is why I have chosen to lean more heavily on the term "unhoused" rather than "homeless" in the context of this book.

Through the practice of direct democracy, these camps can create safe, non-violent environments with some degree of privacy. Each of the case studies presented in this book have established some form of self-governance through regular community meetings where the group adopts basic agreements that, at a minimum, prohibit acts of violence, theft, and illegal drugs within the camp. Those who break the camp's rules are often told to leave, either temporarily or permanently, depending on the offense. The offender typically then has a chance to state his or her case, with a majority vote by the other members determining the outcome.

Because those who break the community agreements are frequently voted out of the camp, these places do not comprehensively address the multi-faceted issue of homelessness. Those with severe addictions and mental complexities will not last long in this kind of organized environment, and other solutions remain necessary for this sector of the chronically homeless. However, the acceptance of organized camps could significantly reduce this population in the future. Not knowing where you will sleep on any given night is enough to drive nearly anyone mad or to resort to vices, and having a secure place to be from the beginning can make all the difference.

These dynamics are shocking to many who presume that the homeless either can't or don't want to organize functionally, but this perception fails to account for several factors that will be revealed in the case studies ahead. The larger theme that unites these places is an inherent sense of egalitarianism—the belief that we are all in this together—that has largely been forgotten by a society focused on self-interest and personal independence. This quality is partly because each person has an equal amount to lose if the camp is evicted, and so everyone does his or her best to maintain a presentable environment.

This intimate practice of democracy is eerily absent elsewhere in the United States, yet most citizens still perceive themselves as members of a democracy. However, the term "democracy" was intentionally left out of both the U.S. Constitution and Declaration of Independence, as the framers found the system, in its true form, impractical—and it's clear that this concern has consistently endured since then. David Graeber writes, "As the history of the past movements all make clear, nothing terrifies those running the U.S. more than the danger of democracy breaking out." He therefore concludes, "If we are to live in any sort of genuinely democratic society, we're going to have to start from scratch."[37] And this is exactly what is taking place in today's tent cities that are being self-organized by the unhoused.

The Occupy Influence

Tent cities have once again entered the public arena since the Occupy Wall Street movement swept the country at the end of 2011. The movement emerged as an effort to raise awareness of the societal consequences of extreme economic inequality, influence the existing federal policies that encouraged this disparity, and build solidarity behind a common cause. In a country that is so commonly influenced by money, Occupy attempted to turn the tables by taking advantage of strength in numbers—pitting 99 percent of Americans against the top 1 percent, and exposing the contradictions of an elite-run "democracy."

Occupy was physically and symbolically embodied in the form of robust protest camps that reclaimed central public spaces in cities throughout the country. Activists descended upon these spaces, packing them with tents and clever signs that illustrated their cause. In addition to the individual tents, makeshift facilities were pieced together to support living full-time at the camp—including kitchens, clinics, libraries, and a variety of other community-based services. While the tent cities popped-up as a demonstration against social and economic inequality, they soon evolved into places of experiment in alternative living. The camps put their political message into practice by operating communities based on direct democracy and horizontal organization. Regular general assembly meetings used consensus decision-making, and they became places where anyone could be sheltered, fed, and heard.

In cities throughout the country, many of the protestors who filled the Occupy camps had experiences that would unintentionally alter the focus of the movement. These places of protest and experiment soon also became places of refuge—providing a stable place to be for the city's homeless. The camps were strikingly similar to those already being organized by the unhoused elsewhere, yet these examples had been largely planned by otherwise housed protestors. For a brief moment in time the housed and the unhoused were living side by side, sharing meals and making decisions together. And as winter set in, inexperienced campers received survival tips from those accustomed to the living situation.[38]

But by the end of December, local authorities had dismantled most camps in some way or another. Cities had been bending their anti-camping ordinances to allow for the protests—directed at larger scale government—but eventually enough was enough, and the great experiment was laid to rest once again. In Portland, the park was cleared of the hundreds of tents that had filled it for over a month, and a fence was erected so that no one could return. A plan to occupy a different space shortly after the eviction was immediately shutdown by the police. Without a physical place the movement lost traction, and with time, the expansive scope of the protest seemed to dissolve back into the various factions that originally composed it.

In the wake of the Occupy camp, the initial focus on federal and global policies shifted to local issues, with many groups coalescing around the issue of homelessness after realizing they had a tangible crisis right in front of them in need of attention. Camp life had deeply impacted several otherwise housed activists, creating a passion for putting this alternative living model back into practice—if not for themselves, at least for their previous neighbors who were now left to fend for themselves. As a result, I would argue that the lessons learned internally in these camps were even more influential than the larger points they voiced externally. Some local Occupy movements—most notably those in Eugene, Madison, and Santa Cruz—have since resurfaced as citizen-driven initiatives for establishing legal "places to be" for the unhoused, adding fuel to an already burning fire.

An Enlightened Vision

By concentrating power in the hands of formal actors, we have not only created a culture of resistance but also a culture of dependence. This depiction is commonly used to stigmatize the homeless, but in reality it is their only legal option. Self-reliant, do-it-yourself approaches to getting oneself out of homelessness, such as the alternative models described in this book, have largely been made illegal. Being independent while being unhoused often results in citations and arrest, making it even more difficult to ever get a job or housing. Instead, the unhoused are forced into top-down social service programs that tend to initiate this culture of dependence—sending the message: you no longer need to know how to take care of yourself in the absence of resources, but at the same time, we don't have the capacity to help you forever. The unhoused are put on a one-way track where they are told: get in line so that you can pay subsidized rent, and not learn how to build your own small home so you don't have to always pay rent.

This message is not new. It has been around since the beginning of American history, dating back to early westward expansion. The white settlers took the land, and in exchange, the indigenous were confined to certain reservations where they could continue to manage the land independently. But with time, the reservations were continually reduced in size as the thirst for expansion continued. With the Dawes Act of 1887, reservations were required to be divided into saleable parcels, which inevitably disrupted indigenous tribal culture by establishing divided and competing interests. Eventually it reached a tipping point—the reservations became so small that there were not enough animals to hunt for food, clothing, or shelter. Cultures that could once exist independently off the land were cut off from their natural provider, and made dependent on commerce. To mitigate this, the white settlers promised to provide for their basic needs in exchange for the land, but never followed through to the extent they claimed. Here, Lakeman's assertion in his history of the grid rings true—cultures that pre-exist the arrival of the grid tend to disappear.

In the late 19th century, General George Custer led a charge to exterminate the Lakota Sioux, resulting in the infamous Battle of Wounded Knee. While at the time this was seen by the public as a necessary means for westward colonial expansion, by the end of the 20th century, Neil Smith argues, "most of us would have to come down on the side of the Sioux." He draws a comparison between the Sioux and today's homeless who "suffer a symbolic extermination and erasure that may leave them alive but struggling on a daily basis to create a life with any quality at all."[39] Smith then makes reference to the Homesteading

Act of 1862, which granted land rights to western pioneers just a few years prior to the massacre of the Sioux. He depicts the early pioneer—commonly portrayed with romantic images of rugged individualism and patriotism—in a much different light:

> ...the majority of heroic pioneers were actually illegal squatters who were democratizing land for themselves. They took the land they needed to make a living, and they organized clubs to defend their land claims against land speculators and land grabbers, established basic welfare circles, and encouraged other squatters to settle because strength lay in numbers.[40]

The key to these early squatters receiving political power was their organization, similar to the tent cities today that have achieved sanctioned status. Smith concludes, "It is just possible that in a future world we may also come to recognize today's squatters are the ones with a more enlightened vision about the urban frontier."[41]

Chapter 3

Tiny Houses

• • •

    While the unhoused are often living simpler, more resource-
ful lives out of necessity, a growing sector of the housed population is
opting to do so by choice. By the turn of the century, the "tiny house
movement" began to capture the heart of America. Since then, more
and more people have taken to the practice of building and living in
radically smaller homes. Building small is certainly nothing new, but it
has only recently begun to be touted as a national movement. There are
now countless blogs documenting and promoting the experience of living in small spaces, and virtually every major media outlet has by now
covered the recent advancement of this lifestyle choice. Once a fixation
particular to counterculture architects and designers, building small has
since become of interest to a broad range of people.

    While on the surface it might seem like a movement defined by
physical form, the structures vary significantly in style, size, and func-
tion. Instead, the common thread behind the movement is a particular
way of life—an ardent dedication to simplicity. This stems not only from
a desire to reduce one's physical footprint on the natural environment,
but also to reap the physiological benefits—the peace of mind that can
result from downsizing one's life. A primary demographic of the move-

ment is young adults who, upon finishing school, prefer their own space yet don't want their freedom tied down by a mortgage. Retiring baby boomers that find themselves with large, high-maintenance houses and empty rooms are also commonly cited as engaging in the movement.[42]

The small houses commonly include a living space, kitchenette, bathroom, a loft for sleeping, and a front porch—typically all in 80 to 200 square feet—and often built on a mobile trailer. Some are hooked up to utilities while others utilize alternative sources of energy and plumbing. They are often quite aesthetically charming, and while this curb appeal attracts diverse and ingenuous admiration, it is actually a very political act. This movement of consuming significantly less stands in direct contrast to the modern interpretation of the American Dream— where material prosperity has come to symbolize success, and where a focus on quantity has become more prevalent than quality.

The Real Housing Problem

The tiny house provides a game-changing perspective to the issue of homelessness. It illustrates that the problem is not so much that some people can't maintain housing, but that our standard of housing has become inaccessible. Today, the average American requires more than three times the amount of space when compared to 1950. Back then, a new single-family house in the U.S. came in at 983 square feet with an average of 3.38 persons per household.[43] But by 2012, the U.S. Census reported that the average new house size had expanded to 2,500 square feet, with an average of only 2.55 persons per household.[44] This means each American apparently now requires about 980 square feet of space *per person*—the same amount that was once sufficient to house the average family. The desire to "keep up with the Joneses" has resulted in more bedrooms, bathrooms, and garages per household, but less people. In fact, many have no people at all. The U.S. Census found that in 2011, 10.1 percent of the housing inventory was vacant (over 13 million units).[45]

Not only does common sense tell us we don't really need this much space, our natural environment is telling us that we *can't* have that much space. The average American is responsible for around 20 tons of CO_2 emissions annually, with residential and commercial buildings alone accounting for 39 percent of total CO_2 emissions in the U.S.—more than any other sector. The most significant factor contributing to our consumption is that these buildings guzzle more than 70 percent of the nation's electricity load.[46] To promote more sustainable practices in the building industry, the U.S. Green Building Council (USGBC) was established in 1993. The organization points to the built environment's impact on climate change as the primary incentive for change:

> Scientists predict that left unchecked, emission of CO_2 and other greenhouse gases from human activities will raise global temperatures by 2.5°F to 10°F this century. The effects will be profound, and may include rising sea levels, more frequent floods and droughts, and increased spread of infectious diseases. To address the threat of climate change, greenhouse gas emissions must be slowed, stopped, and reversed. Meeting the challenge will require dramatic advances in technologies and a shift in how the world economy generates and uses technology.[47]

Sustainable building certification systems—such as the LEED program developed by the USGBC—have been formed in an attempt to encourage this shift. However, some have argued that these certification programs only appear to be "greening" the status quo rather than catalyzing substantial change.[48] The programs use a point tallying system to reward the implementation of sustainable features, which still incentivizes an additive process that caters to the building industry. For example, emphasis is placed on making lighting, heating, and cooling systems more efficient rather than reducing the overall demand by simply building smaller homes. To account for this, LEED has since added a "home size adjustor" that requires homes larger than the average size to earn more points, and reduces the requirements for homes below the average size. But still, under this framework, a 6,000 square foot house for two people can still be certified as sustainable if it adds enough "green" bells and whistles. The house may be more energy efficient than a similar sized conventional house, but there is still an enormous amount of space to maintain. Even if it is a net-zero house, think about how much energy had to be used to convert raw materials into the house. This is not meant to understate the importance of efficiency and technological advancement, but to emphasize that it must be paired with a more practical standard of living.

A recent study by the Oregon Department of Environmental Quality (DEQ) demonstrates how the existing certification systems significantly undervalue the importance of size. In an evaluation of 25 different green building practices over the lifecycle of a home, the DEQ found that reducing the size of the home is in fact the single most effective measure for reducing its impact on the environment. The study found that a medium sized home (2,262 square feet) built to Energy Star standards—which includes more efficient windows, doors, insulation, and air tightness—reduced emissions by 15 percent when compared to the same sized house built to standard code. However, it was revealed that simply reducing the size of the standard built home to 1,633 square feet would achieve even greater savings.[49] This is because it is the only practice that reduces both energy usage *and* material demand. Using fewer materials also means that there is less energy used in making and transporting the necessary materials. This may all seem intuitive, but it is often lost in the hype around other, sexier green building practices.

Building small is certainly effective, but it also demands drastically downsizing our material expectations. Surely this is not for everyone, but the ever growing tiny house movement—and the environmental and social consciousness that it signifies—takes this practice to the extreme. It represents the return of pragmatism to the equation of the American Dream for some, where the desire for quality once again prevails over quantity.

Tiny Houses & The Code

Rethinking the American Dream takes more than just a shift in cultural norms, though, since consumption is not entirely optional when it comes to home building. Most tiny houses are not technically legal as primary dwellings due to many of the same minimum standards that made SROs obsolete in the second part of the twentieth century. As stated in the last chapter, it makes sense to regulate profit-driven

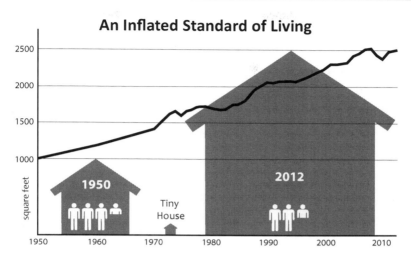

The average size of a new single-family house has risen sharply in the U.S. while the average persons per household has dropped.

Note: missing data between 1951-1959 and 1961-1969

Source: U.S. Census Bureau

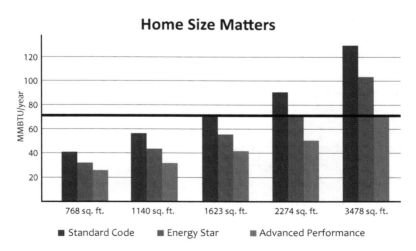

In a study of 25 green building practices, the Oregon DEQ found building small to be the single most effective measure for reducing environmental impact.

Source: Oregon DEQ

developers—but what if an individual prefers a small space? What if it is all they can afford? And what if, like many involved in the tiny house movement, they want to build it themselves? Kern, Kogon, and Thallon call attention to how the enforcement of the building code has expanded beyond its original intent:

> It is important to recognize that the safeguards of the codes were originally intended as an edict to builders whose product was destined for use by others. The codes were not originally intended to inhibit people from building shelters designed for their own occupancy. It was assumed that, in providing for their own needs, owner-builders would do everything within their means to insure their own comfort and safety. The breakdown of caveat emptor was not the result of people doing for themselves. If the codes were indeed designed to protect the consumer, it is ludicrous for building departments to intractably hold the letter of the law over those builders who are, in fact, the consumer. In this instance, we have the situation of people being 'protected' from themselves by government agencies.[50]

A larger irony is that, while buildings codes were intended to protect the consumer from the builder, the codes have essentially been written by the building industry. Local municipalities enact codes that are handed down by the state, and the states adopt national models crafted by private organizations. Historically, these organizations have been heavily influenced and mobilized by the building and insurance industries. For example, the first national building code was written in 1905 by the National Board of Fire Underwrites, as an effort by the fire insurance industry to reduce risk and loss resulting from widespread urban fires.[51] For most of the twentieth century, three regional building codes—the Uniform Build Code used on the West Coast, the BOCA National Building Code used on the East Coast and Midwest, and the Standard Building Code used in the Southeast—were adopted to eliminate variations among cities. Then, in 2000, the three organizations merged to form the International Code Council, forming a single standard—the International Building Code (IBC)—for the entire nation.

In setting out to legally build a small house, following all of the building code and permitting requirements results in proportionally high costs and standards that make it difficult to simplify one's lifestyle. With sufficient finances, modifications can be made to meet requirements around insulation, utilities, permanent foundations, and loft spaces—though it surely defeats the intent of this alternative. For example, insulation requirements are currently standardized regardless of the size of the house, even though small houses require significantly less energy to heat. This necessitates 2x6 wall framing when 2x4 is structurally sound. This burden has recently been recognized by the Oregon DEQ in their effort to incentivize the adoption of small homes, and they have since proposed size-based tiers where energy efficiency standards are a variable of house size. However, minimum square footage requirements for a habitable space are still a major limiting factor for very small homes. The absolute minimum established by the IBC is to have at least one room of 120 square feet and no room that is less than 7 feet wide (except for bathroom and kitchen). To be considered a dwelling, it must also have additional square footage for a kitchen and bathroom. However, many municipalities have additional provisions that further restrict minimum house size.

As a result, the tiny house movement has witnessed a number of notable figures rise in the media, demonstrating that safety, welfare, and sanitation—the vanguard of the building code—are not dependent upon size. In 1998, Sarah Susanka wrote her best-selling book *The Not So Big House*, which makes the argument that a sense of home has almost nothing to do with quantity and everything to do with quality. The book's popularity has led to a lengthy series on this topic. In 2002, Jay Shafer co-founded the Small House Society and started Tumbleweed Tiny House Company—an early manufacturer of the tiny house movement. He quickly became the iconic figure behind the movement, appearing with his self-built houses on virtually every major news source. Since then, there have been a number of others to develop a cult following on the Internet—including Dee Williams of "Portland Alternative Dwellings," Derek Diedricksen's "Relax Shacks," Tammy Strobel's "Rowdy Kittens," Andrew Odom's "Tiny r(E)volution," and Kent Griswold's "Tiny House Blog"—just to name a few of what appears to be a growing list of tiny house celebrities. Their specialties range from tiny house design to commentary on simple living to documenting the scope of the movement.

Loopholes

For now, the tiny house movement is still heavily dependent upon loopholes. The most popular approach has been to build the small structures on trailers, which puts the tiny house under the jurisdiction of the DMV rather than the building department. While there are still hoops to jump through, they are more reasonable, and some suggest this is because the regulations have not been guided by the housing industry. However, this option still presents a legal predicament: Going the DMV route requires registering your house as a trailer, RV, or mobile home. While there is some degree of local variance here, in general you can't live in a trailer, an RV can only remain on a site for a limited amount of time, and a mobile home can only be placed within a site zoned as a mobile home park. The most beaten path here is to register the structure as an RV and park it on private, residential land—often in the backyard of a friend or family member. The house can then usually remain there indefinitely, as long as no one makes a formal complaint.

The other alternative is the "auxiliary" route. While the size limit varies depending on the state, most codes allow structures under a certain area to be exempt from permitting and inspection, with the understanding that they are for storage purposes rather than living in. But many cities have witnessed an underground phenomenon where homeowners are building tiny houses in their backyards under the cover of a glorified garden shed. In fact, this option is likely much more common than the trailer approach, but significantly less publicized because it is not technically legal to live in for any period of time, and more difficult to move if you are cited. Some property owners have even taken the route of renting out their primary dwelling and moving into a tiny house in their backyard. These escape artists can still declare that they are simply sharing the primary dwelling for formal purposes. But, similar to the RV loophole, the practicality of this approach is once again largely dependent upon avoiding complaints from neighbors.

The simplified lifestyle embodied by the tiny house movement will certainly not appeal to everyone, but it is clear that there is growing support. Unfortunately, our governing bodies have not kept pace with this shift in building ideology as a result of larger forces at play. In many cities, those pursuing this lifestyle are often pushed to the margins or off the grid completely due to strict zoning regulations and building codes. While some might prefer this solitude, the trouble with the trailer and auxiliary approach is that people are quietly avoiding the legal issue rather than confronting the fact that a sector of the American population prefers tiny house living. It is a housing trend in the shadows that is going completely untracked by census data.

The cult-following on social media sites makes clear that there is not only a growing amount of tiny house dwellers, but also an enormous amount of tiny house lurkers—people intrigued by the possibility but watching from the sidelines for now—many of whom might pursue it but are uncomfortable living in a legal grey area. If people want to build and live small, we need to fight for the right to do so. Just as the unhoused are in a fight to establish a meager space of their own, the housed are in a fight for the right to live a simpler life. If both sides succeed, we could witness the emergence of more equitable and sustainable communities—blurring the line between the housed and the unhoused and redefining home.

Keep it Simple

As a primary leader of the tiny house movement, Jay Shafer's building philosophy has been influential in shaping how these little structures have come to be built and who is pursuing them. "I figure that if the house you're creating is very small," Shafer writes, "you might as well put some of the time and money saved on square footage into good design and quality materials."[52] As a result, his own tiny house is the cheapest house in Sonoma County, but on the other hand, it is also the most expensive per square foot. The base price for a finished structure from Tumbleweed Tiny House Company (which Shafer founded but has since departed from) starts at around $60,000. But, with the tiny house, most costs are upfront. Shafer points out that square footage is one of the cheapest things you can add to a house, but the long-term costs of heating, cooling, and maintaining a large space are high. While material demand is reduced overall, the classic tiny house tries to pack all of the core elements and conveniences of the modern house into a very small space—contributing to the high cost per square foot. In addition, the structures are often finished with ornate detail and add-ons that charm the spectator and appeal to high-end clients.

> The classic image of a tiny home is a grown-up dollhouse, a spot to play make-believe. The scale is humble, but the architectural detail is rich: eyebrow windows, stick-style trusses. This is the jewel box you'll see on a website like Jay Shafer's Four Lights Tiny House Company or in a dream-book like Lloyd Kahn's "Tiny Homes: Simple Shelter." It stands somewhere on a lost coast, or in a hermit's hollow: private Edens, places you'd like to be.[53]

This philosophy appeals to those consciously downsizing from larger homes, but what about those on the brink of losing their existing house or apartment? What about those already going without housing? If you are building small, my natural inclination would be just the opposite of Shafer's: you might as well try to make it as affordable and accessible as possible. This philosophy arose largely out of my interest in self-organized tent cities—since the tiny house was an ideal vehicle for improving the physical infrastructure of the camps without disrupting the existing social balance of privacy and community. But in order to realize something like this, we need to first consider the tiny house on a shoestring budget.

I do not at all mean to trivialize the importance of the classic tiny house as a mode of downsizing from larger, unsustainable living spaces. After all, it is a rather ingenious way to get members of the middle-class to reduce their carbon footprint since it still includes access to many of the modern conveniences they have become accustomed to, but on a much smaller scale. Rather, I am arguing that the breadth of the movement should also emphasize the potential of tiny housing as a mode of upsizing as well—from tents to basic, affordable tiny houses. By including both ends of the spectrum—those downsizing and those upsizing—we can restore a very low-cost housing option that appeals to a vibrant mix of people. This offers a new take on the early SROs, which attracted a wide-range of tenants in pursuit of an economical option that preserved privacy and autonomy. In the face of climate change, we can now add those in pursuit of an ecological option to the mix as well.

The Tiny House on a Shoestring Budget

◊ <u>Build it yourself:</u> The most significant way to lower the cost is to build a tiny house yourself, though everyone does not possess the skills required to take this on. The tiny house does, however, put this possibility back within the grasp of more people by simplifying the construction process. A number of resources can be found online that teach novice builders the basic skills necessary for building your own small home. Even if you can't complete the entire job yourself, it is often possible to enlist some volunteer labor for a good-natured project such as this.

◊ <u>Be economically creative:</u> A more economical structure can be achieved by minimizing the amount of materials necessary to complete the structure while still ensuring that it is structurally sound. This takes good design with a functional reason for each material used. Being flexible and utilizing recycled and discounted materials is another useful strategy. However, this is not to say you should settle for an unattractive shed made from rotting lumber. Aesthetics are key. In fact, I would argue that it is the tiny house movement's strongest asset in appealing to the larger community. But with a little creativity, this can be achieved without excessive and costly materials.

◊ <u>Skip the trailer:</u> The trailer is typically the single most expensive component of the tiny house, and many people include it simply as a means to avert building code violations rather than by choice. There is certainly value in the transportability that a trailer offers,

Affordable Tiny House A | 120 sq. ft.

Roof

Loft

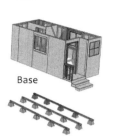

Base

Foundation

Affordable Tiny House B | 144 sq. ft.

Roof

Loft

Base

Foundation

Backyard Bungalows | www.backyardbungalows.net

but unless you plan to move your house regularly, setting the structure on raised pier blocks is an alternative that can achieve similar flexibility at a fraction of the cost. With this method, the tiny house can be easily lifted onto a trailer and transported if necessary without each structure requiring its own.

◊ Share Facilities: The tiny house movement is founded on the notion of simplifying one's life, yet too often these little structures seem to try to cram every feature of the modern house into a very small space. The common tendency of mounting these little structures on trailers seems to have warped their development to model the independence of the American RV culture. But we don't necessarily need to fit every feature into every structure. Some functions, such as the kitchen and bathroom, can be shared by living in communities of tiny houses or by utilizing a larger, primary dwelling on the property. With a focus on simplicity, sharing facilities makes sense and dramatically reduces costs.

◊ Build a Village: Sharing facilities not only reduces costs, but also provides a feasible method for legally developing tiny house communities. By placing several tiny houses on the same property with shared facilities, the development can be classified as a "congregate living facility"—similar to college dormitories or assisted living centers. Under this interpretation, the tiny house is distinguished as a "sleeping unit"—a space that can provide provisions for sleeping, living, eating, and either cooking or sanitation but not both—rather than a "dwelling unit," which has much more stringent code regulations. The result is a more flexible living space where the tiny house becomes an independent residence dependent upon a surrounding village.

Chapter 4

From Camp to Village

• • •

Tent cities are almost always approached from a tragic, signs of the times point of view—both by advocates and the news media. But my interest was piqued for different reasons. I found the crisis was not simply that people were living in these conditions, but that people were *not being allowed* to live in these conditions without the provision of any alternative. I was captured by the visual potency of the story, but not because tent cities alluded to how bad things are. I was attracted to them because they presented a striking opportunity—a foundation for a self-managed, human-scale model of low-cost and low-impact housing.

Planning school had left me pessimistic about the formal planning process. It always seemed to hopelessly end in ubiquitous, sterile spaces of inequity, even with the best of intentions. Christopher Alexander brilliantly captures the essence of this dilemma when he describes how "order of organic process" has been replaced by "artificial order of control"—making it impossible to build an environment that is "alive." He argues that the only way to build an "alive" environment is through "piecemeal growth," where meager beginnings undergo a reparative process, constantly evolving in reaction to existing conditions.[54]

While much of the planning field has accepted these ideas by now, they have failed to be implemented due to larger forces. Piecemeal growth might sound nice, but existing power structures systematically shred just about any hope of it. Complete plans and permits are required before any construction may begin. Buildings must be completely finished before any person ever inhabits them. This is a process that caters to mass-produced subdivisions and superblocks that are built to be consumed.

The informal nature of the self-organized camps that I observed offers a stark contrast to this process. Operating under exceptional circumstances of emergency, these settlements are sometimes able to avoid the reach of formal planning. In doing so, these democratic communities become optimal grounds for starting from scratch with a more human approach to planning. Self-organized tent cities serve as an example of how the unhoused are, out of necessity, collectively finding solutions to their own problems in their day-to-day struggle for survival. As a result, their communities embody the piecemeal growth described by Alexander. Formal actors often refer to this as unplanned development. But all communities are planned to some extent. The difference is in who is doing the planning. The residents of the self-organized camp are making decisions that directly impact their physical and social organization, and in doing so they are rediscovering key aspects of a sustainable community—most notably self-management, direct democracy, tolerance, and resourceful strategies for living with less. These characteristics not only address many of the shortfalls of traditional responses to poverty, but also the narrow scope of conventional housing practices.

By combining the curb appeal and general romanticism around the tiny house with the self-organized tent cities introduced in Chapter 1, we find a marketable solution—one that transcends the stigma of the camp to the optimism and vitality of a village. Through the lens of an urban planner, I have documented a variety of alternative forms of emergency shelter already being carried out by the unhoused, and position these informal settlements as a point of departure on which to build. The positive social dynamics of these informal communities—chiefly their ability to balance the need for stability, security, autonomy, privacy, and community—are combined with an improved physical infrastructure to present an alternative model for transitional and affordable housing. It is a model that begins with the most basic right of providing shelter for oneself in the absence of other alternatives, and connects with the notion that local control and participation are central to creating a truly sustainable community. It is a village model.

The Village Model

For much of human history the village was the primary form of settlement. Traditionally, the village had a limited population (around 5-30 families) in compact clusters of dwellings surrounded by agricultural farmland that supported the population. The development was geomorphic and the layout accommodated defense, socialization, and a high degree of self-sufficiency. Transient villages existed early on, based on the availability of resources, though most became permanent settlements with the establishment of long-distance trade. But with the Industrial Revolution came the transition from the village to the town, and eventually the city, and the term "village" has since become ambiguous and distorted. Today, at least in the United States, most commonly it is ironically used in branding consumer development—sprawling subdivision "village," commercial shopping strip "village," or ubiquitous apartment complex "village"—all of which exhibit patterns that inherently contradict the traditional concept. These spaces consistently lack the sense of place that once defined the village, and instead focus on efficiency and consumption. The heavy use of the term in branding can be attributed to its marketability—the idea that the village is culturally symbolic of a place we all want to experience—rather than any direct relation to the traditional settlement pattern.

So, moving forward, let's take a more thoughtful look at what a village model can offer within today's urban context by exploring a few aspects of the concept:

◊ Physical: The village combines a sense of ownership over a small, private space with an abundance of shared commons. It spreads the functions of the modern house into separate structures, which better connects people to their natural and social environment.

◊ Social: The concept is based on the premise that local control and broad participation are central to creating a sustainable community, and that social isolation is the root of many of the problems we face as a society. The village returns to small-scale, democratic communities where each voice has value and social capital is the primary economic engine of change.

◊ Economic: Since the 1950s we have more than tripled the amount of space that we believe an individual needs. The village reduces our inflated standards of living and returns to a human-scale form of development that is affordable and economically sustainable.

◊ Ecological: In the face of climate change and peak oil, the village presents a way forward that dramatically reduces human impact on the natural environment by minimizing, localizing, and sharing resources. It looks to renewable forms of energy and embraces living with less.

From Camp To Village

This progression from camp to village that I have been referring to is not without precedent. The concept was first pioneered by Los Angeles' Dome Village, which was legally established in 1993. Here, a shantytown transformed into a village of 20 geodesic domes, designed by a student of Buckminster Fuller. The self-governing community housed up to 34 individuals and families with a focus on those who refused to stay in traditional homeless shelters.

The next, and probably most well known example came when Portland's Camp Dignity was sanctioned as Dignity Village in 2001 on city-owned land. This organically democratic community of around 60 members has attracted visitors from across the globe, and has been influential in inspiring the examples that follow. In 2004, Fresno's Village of Hope was established, though with more austere rules and accommodations than its predecessor. And in 2009 Ventura's River Haven community transitioned from tents to 19 U-Domes provided by World Shelters, but also incorporates more stringent requirements.

The next inception of a sincere village model did not occur until Eugene's Opportunity Village and Olympia's Quixote Village opened in 2013, both on public land. The concept has since emerged from the Northwest to inspire projects like Madison's OM Village, Ithaca's Second Wind Cottages, and Austin's Community First Village—all currently in the planning or development stages—and is being pursued by advocate groups throughout the country.

So, five years after the onslaught of media attention that highlighted tent cities as symbols of our nation's failure, we are now beginning to see stories of hope. We are seeing a grassroots movement that is gaining traction in the effort to address this very same dilemma. Through partnerships between the unhoused and housed the tiny house village is gradually being accepted. It is truly the start of an American success story, where citizens recognized a problem and have responded with local, community-based solutions.

In an article carried throughout the U.S. and in London, the *Associated Press* reported: "There's a growing effort across the nation from advocates and religious groups to build these compact buildings because they are cheaper than a traditional large-scale shelter, help the recipients socially because they are built in communal settings and are environmentally friendly due to their size."[55] *Yes!* magazine reported: "A growing number of towns and cities have found a practical solution to homelessness through the construction of tiny-house villages—and housing officials are taking notice."[56] The U.S. Department of Housing and Urban Development (HUD) has even endorsed the model as a viable solution stating: "It's certainly something that we would encourage other communities to take a look at when it comes to creating solutions for housing the chronically homeless… It's a very important step in terms of the kinds of services we should be providing to people that need assistance."[57]

This book intends to serve as a platform for advocates, professionals, students, city officials, and community leaders with an interest in establishing a similar village model. A trail has been blazed by these early projects, and now it is up to others to make it happen in all corners of the country. Unlike conventional development it is not something that can just be stamped—it takes a village to build a village.

OM VILLAGE | Madison, Wisconsin

Following the dismantling of the Occupy Madison camp, OM Build was formed as an initiative to construct tiny houses for those experiencing homelessness. The structures are 98 square feet and cost around $5,000 each to build with volunteer labor. Recipients of the tiny houses are expected to contribute a certain number of hours toward the construction of their house. At under 3,000 pounds in total weight and mounted on a trailer, the structures are street legal without registration—though local regulations require they move every 48 hours.

Inspired by similar projects in Portland and Eugene, OM Village was conceived as a permanent place to park nine of these tiny houses and build a community. The plan was approved—after a lengthy public process—as a planned unit development (PUD) for a former gas station and auto-body shop. The existing structure will be adaptively reused as a building workshop and will also host common facilities to support the tiny houses around it.

> Although city staff advised the Plan Commission not to consider the socioeconomic aspects of the proposal, it did seem to weigh into commissioners' leniency with the zoning code. "My head might say that this doesn't meet all the standards and we're not quite there. My heart says it's worth a shot," commissioner Michael Heifetz said.[58]

Tiny house in front of state capital building; Photo provided by OM Build

From House to Village

While the tiny house movement offers an ideal scale of housing for the progression from camp to village, it lacks the social foundation present in the self-organized tent city. Tiny house experiments are typically geographically isolated from one another, and communication among tiny house dwellers is primarily a digital experience. Design strategies and construction plans are sold as downloadable e-books and PDFs rather than shared among neighbors. However, more recent trends show the movement is emerging from the cybersphere and gaining a more physical presence with the emergence of a number of hands-on tiny house workshops and the first tiny house conference in 2014.

Many tiny house advocates have recognized this shortfall, and the lack of these kind of villages is not by choice—building codes and zoning regulations have consistently frustrated individual efforts to accommodate congregations of the classic tiny house. Boneyard Studios in Washington, DC may be the best existing example, which hosts a handful of tiny houses on a single urban lot. But for now it is merely a "demonstration site"—showing what *could* be—since existing regulations still prohibit full-time occupancy.

The transitional and affordable villages described in this book have and will transpire first because they are connected with a larger cause that positively addresses a highly visible and vocalized political issue in many cities. But through the acceptance of these tiny house villages oriented at taking up the issue of homelessness, it has pried open the door to accepting tiny house developments for other demographics as well.

While the village is a new frontier for the tiny house movement, the concept has been tried and tested in other shadows of the housing market. Both cohousing and eco-villages can offer inspiration and guidance to these budding movements by both the housed and unhoused. They provide precedent for unconventional trends in development for establishing community-based housing—though not without difficulties of their own. In the remainder of this chapter, I will turn to both individually to see what they can offer in defining an alternative framework for sustainable living.

Cohousing

Detached single-family housing was designed with the nuclear family in mind. But while demographics have shifted to include fewer people in homes with a greater diversity of household types, our housing options have remained practically unchanged. One major difference is the increase in one and two person households—including single parents, married couples with no children, and single households—which suggests the need to downsize the prevalence of the single-family house and move beyond suburbia. Consequently, cohousing has emerged as a response to our limited housing options to put forth a new type of housing with our changing society in mind.

In cohousing, private residences are usually clustered together similar to a condominium or townhouse development. However, the built environment is based around a few basic design strategies that set it apart. This includes separating the car from the residence, connecting residences instead with pathways, and centrally locating common facilities. Emphasis is placed on making front porches an extension of the home, and orienting the most active parts of the house—such as the kitchen—toward the walking paths and shared open space. All of these elements are designed to encourage social interaction within the community. But at the same time, cohousing also respects the desire for autonomy and privacy. It is based on a private ownership structure much like conventional housing, and the idea is that each resident can choose to participate in the community as much or as little as they like. But what usually draws people to cohousing is a desire for a more practical and sustainable lifestyle to share with others.

A primary point here is that cohousing marks a trend toward smaller dwellings with shared, common facilities among people who are securely housed. The demographics of cohousing are diverse and intergenerational—including retiring baby boomers, seniors, newly married couples, and average families. Kathryn McCamant and Chuck Durrett—the architects credited with bringing the cohousing concept from Europe to the United States—note, "we have seen the average size of private residences within cohousing communities shrink dramatically; between 1975 and 2010, it has gone down by nearly one half, as family size shrank and people learned to use the community's kids' room, the workshop space, and the other common facilities as an extension of their private house."[59] The most defining aspect of a cohousing community is the common house, where residents can cook and share meals together. Each residence still has its own smaller kitchen, but by sharing larger facilities individuals can be more resourceful—reducing consumption while improving social connectivity.

Another key aspect of cohousing is the emphasis on a participatory design process. Unlike conventional development, cohousing is planned and designed by the initial members of the community—typically with varying degrees of assistance from professionals. McCamant and Durrett have facilitated this process for dozens of cohousing projects, and they find it accomplishes two significant goals: it builds both consensus around finalizing the design of the development and relationships among the people that will make and sustain the community. Participatory design can create a sense of ownership that encourages residents to actively engage in maintaining the community into the distant future. Unlike residential subdivisions, cohousing developments are self-managed by the residents from the beginning. But similar to the pursuit of sanctioned camps and villages for the unhoused, the unconventional nature of cohousing often faces significant NIMBY opposition—specifically around concerns of density and adjacent property value.

Through leading workshops and witnessing the finished products, McCamant and Durrett have learned a lot about what works and what doesn't. Of particular interest in the context of this book is community size. Cohousing developments commonly range from 8 to 35 households. McCamant and Durrett have found that large communities (26 to 35 households) offer the benefit of diversity and more extensive facilities through economy of scale, but run the risk of taking on an institutional feel where the individual lacks voice. On the other end of the spectrum, they have found that small communities (8 to 15 households) are less complicated, less formal, and less likely to attract NIMBY opposition. However, fewer people make it more difficult to manage a community, and also less cost-effective since many development costs are fixed regardless of size. As a result, they advocate for a range somewhere in between (16 to 25 households): "To make a case for the medium size is to make a case for cohousing itself—large enough to have extensive shared facilities, but small enough to be easily managed by direct democracy."[60]

In a way, what I am advocating in this book is a form of cohousing—focused toward creating transitional and affordable housing communities. While cohousing is typically more economical than the conventional housing market, there is plenty of room to make it more affordable to very low-income individuals and families. By reducing the size of private dwellings even further and increasing dependence on common facilities, we can create a low-cost alternative while maintaining the values of autonomy and privacy sought out by residents of today's self-organized tent cities and yesterday's SRO hotels. This kind of approach bucks the trend of current practices for responding to poverty, which tend to alienate the individual as part of the process of upward mobility.

Eco-villages

Eco-villages represent a convergence of people with a simplified, ecological standard of living. While the residents of cohousing value community and usually share a concern for the environment, the eco-village provides a model for more radical, comprehensive change in this regard. Cohousing is sometimes seen as a component of an eco-village, which tends to further emphasize agriculture, energy and water usage, and commercial activities as well. It is more than just another type of housing—an eco-village is an alternative lifestyle that strives toward minimal impact on the land, a high degree of self-sufficiency, and strengthening social bonds.

In pursuing these goals, the communities are most often located in rural areas where land is more plentiful and less regulated. Urban and suburban examples must creatively adapt to more restrictive regulations, resulting in a wide variety of forms that do not always resemble the traditional understanding of a village. For example, a multi-family complex in a dense urban area can be renovated by a group of like-minded residents to include more sustainable features—such as Los Angeles Eco-village—or a group of adjacent single-family housing parcels can be retrofitted and infilled with accessory dwelling units—such as Maitreya Eco-village in Eugene.

Similar to "tent city," the types of settlements that the term "eco-village" encompasses are far-reaching. The common thread between the various examples is that each self-identifies as an eco-village. This loose definition is intentional in order to be inclusionary of diverse and experimental communities using ecological principles to live as light on the land as possible. A popular definition is "a human-scale, full-featured settlement in which human activities are harmlessly integrated into the natural world in a way that is supportive of healthy human development and can be successfully continued into the indefinite future"—though this is just meant to be a starting point.[61] Eco-villages have a foundation built on three dimension—ecological, social, and personal—and the degree to which a community balances the emphasis on these dimensions is what makes each unique.

By now, it should be clear that the tent cities and villages included in this book already demonstrate strong personal and social dimensions. In progressing from camp to village, the addition of an ecological dimension can help break down stereotypes and build relationships. Taking advantage of free, natural systems through grey water collection, composting toilets, solar showers, organic gardens, or natural building techniques are just a few common elements of eco-villages that could be applied to improve physical conditions and increase self-sufficiency. This could both reduce the stigma around dependency held by conservatives, and further appeal to progressives interested in sustainable living.

A key difference in this comparison is that eco-villages are places of choice while self-organized tent cities—though autonomous in nature—are places of necessity. Consequently, the unhoused are often more apt to live sustainable lifestyles than the average citizen since they are accustomed to being resourceful and participating in an alternative, close-knit social organization. I have found that this experience, though initially unintentional, has led many to develop a more egalitarian outlook that is conducive to living in community.

As a result, the two are natural allies and could mutually benefit from partnering. At the simplest level, eco-villages could provide political support to a local tent city as a viable alternative to conventional housing. Additionally, members of the tent city could become involved at the eco-village, learning practical skills to apply in their own community. While eco-villages expand their cause and the scope of sustainable living, members of tent cities could learn how to build and heat small, eco-minded dwellings and reduce their dependence on city-provided utilities.

Sustainable Living

As the triple crises of climate change, peak oil, and economic upheaval continue to manifest themselves globally, the status quo will continue to be challenged, requiring a drastic evolution in the forms of human settlement. Even if alternative energy sources emerge, so far scientists and researchers have found that none would come close to supporting our current standard of living and development now supported by oil. A plausible scenario, then, will include the necessity to live in more interdependent communities, which stands in direct contradiction to modern values of individualism and globalization.

> Access to endless amounts of cheap energy made us rich, and wrecked our climate, and it also made us the first people on earth who had no practical need of our neighbors... In the halcyon days of the final economic booms, everyone on your cul de sac could have died overnight from some mysterious plague, and while you might have been sad, you wouldn't have been inconvenienced. Our economy, unlike any that came before it, is designed to work without the input of your neighbors.[62]

Consequently many have concluded that we feel more alone now than ever. This lack of social capital and reciprocity in American communities has resulted in a people who are "disconnected from family, friends, neighbors, and our democratic structures."[63] This is why Bill Mollison—co-founder of the field of permaculture—argues, "We need well-designed villages today more than any other enterprise: villages to relocate those soon-to-be refugees from sea-level rise, villages to house people from urban slums, and villages where people of like-mind can find someone to talk to and work with."[64] Tiny houses, cohousing, and eco-villages provide precedent of substantial progress in this direction, but all face major roadblocks by urban policies designed to keep unconventional practices on the fringe. But through addressing the emergency of homelessness, we find a backdoor to implementing these sustainable alternatives that opens with the key of low-cost solutions to a high-profile problem.

Thus far, only those with strong convictions around the state of our social and ecological environment are pursuing sustainable living alternatives. Less intensive modifications are being made to the conventional housing stock to increase energy efficiency, but the success here can often be attributed to the fact that these alterations reduce monthly bills without compromising existing standards of living. Most are only willing to compromise the comforts of their current lifestyle to a certain extent when left to choice. So, what better opportunity exists to expand sustainable living now than to incorporate those residing in tents, the most basic shelter? We must reestablish the bottom end of the housing market to reduce the direct and indirect costs of homelessness, but we must do so in a way that diverges from the environmental consequences of our conventional housing stock. We must address homelessness and sustainability together.

Through this pursuit of transitional and affordable villages, we find a housing alternative that is economically, socially, and environmentally sustainable while meeting the common desire for autonomy and privacy. This is accomplished through combining compact, private spaces with an abundance of shared resources. It emphasizes democratic control, where residents themselves determine community issues and each is free to decide how his or her life should proceed. It is an alternative intended not just for the homeless, but also for those wanting to devote a smaller percentage of their income toward housing, those wanting a better connection with their neighbors, and those wanting to reduce their environmental footprint. It is a model for the future.

PART II | CAMPS

PART II | CAMPS

THE JUNGLE

ITHICA, NY

1940s-2013

▲▲▲▲▲▲▲▲▲▲

Status: unsanctioned | uninterrupted until eviction in 2013 | some have returned

Site: private land (railroad company) | 100+ year history of camps on this site

TENT CITY

NASHVILLE, TN

1980s-2010

▲▲▲▲

▲▲▲▲▲▲▲▲▲▲▲▲▲▲▲▲▲▲▲▲▲▲▲▲▲▲▲▲▲▲▲▲

Status: unsanctioned | forced evacuation by flood | site condemned

Site: state DOT land | flood zone

TENT CITY 3 & 4

SEATTLE, WA

2000-present / 2004-present

▲▲▲▲▲▲▲▲▲▲▲▲▲▲▲▲▲▲▲▲▲▲ *each*

Status: sanctioned | itinerant

Site: rotates among various church land at 3 month intervals

CAMP QUIXOTE

OLYMPIA, WA

2007-2013

▲▲▲▲▲▲

Status: sanctioned | itinerant | closed with the opening of Quixote Village

Site: rotated among various church land at 3-6 month intervals

PINELLAS HOPE

ST. PETERSBURG, FL

2007-present

▲▲▲▲▲▲▲▲▲▲▲▲▲▲▲

▲▲▲▲▲▲▲▲▲▲▲▲▲▲▲▲▲▲▲▲▲▲▲▲▲▲▲▲▲▲

▲▲▲▲▲▲▲

Status: sanctioned | permanent

Site: private land (Catholic Diocese) | unincorporated | 11 miles from city center

CAMP TAKE NOTICE

ANN ARBOR, MI

2008-2012

▲▲▲▲▲▲▲▲▲▲▲▲▲▲

Status: unsanctioned | evicted | pursuing a planned unit development

Site: various public & private land | state DOT land for 2+ years

▲ = 5 Tents

NICKELSVILLE   2008-present
SEATTLE, WA

▲▲▲▲▲▲▲▲▲▲▲▲▲▲▲▲▲▲▲▲▲▲▲▲▲▲

Status: unsanctioned | evicted & split into two separate camps in 2013
Site: over a dozen other short-term locations | city-owned land for 2+ years)

CAMP RUNAMUCK & HOPE CITY   2009-2010
PROVIDENCE, RI

▲▲▲▲▲▲▲▲▲▲▲▲▲▲▲▲▲▲▲▲▲▲▲▲▲▲▲▲▲▲
Status: unsanctioned | evicted   ▲▲▲▲▲▲▲▲
Site: public land (city park)

CAMP HOPE   2011-present
LAS CRUCES, NM

▲▲▲▲▲▲▲▲▲

Status: sanctioned | permanent | rezoned as part of planned unit development
Site: private land (non-profit)

RIGHT 2 DREAM TOO   2011-present
PORTLAND, OR

▲▲▲▲▲▲ *+ 60 rest area spaces*
Status: unsanctioned | seeking sanctioned site
Site: private land (individual) | central location

HANGTOWN HAVEN   2012-2013
PLACERVILLE, CA

▲▲▲▲▲▲▲▲

Status: sanctioned | temporary use permit not renewed
Site: private land (individual)

WHOVILLE   2013-2014
EUGENE, OR

▲▲▲▲▲▲▲

Status: unsanctioned | evicted
Site: various public land throughout city

▲ = *5 Tents*

Chapter 5

Ann Arbor's Sanctuary Camp

• • •

**What are the dynamics of an unsanctioned,
self-organized tent city?**

The City of Ann Arbor's Master Plan aims to provide a vision forward in an effort to guide decision-makers, stating, "The quality of life in Ann Arbor will be characterized by its diversity, beauty, vibrancy and livability and ultimately will depend upon the positive interaction of these systems." Given these standards, it seems strange that the local tent city, known as "Camp Take Notice," is altogether missing from the plan. The camp had been in existence in some form or another since the fall of 2008. Despite being displaced to various locations throughout the city, the formal process took little notice.

The camp's origin can be traced to Caleb Poirier, a native of the city, who became homeless shortly after losing his job as a paramedic due to unrelenting medical conditions. Ashamed of his situation, he made his way to Seattle in order to distance himself from the family and friends in his hometown. During this time he experienced living in two sanctioned tent cities ("Tent City 3" and "Tent City 4" which are described in Chapter 7) and soon became a dedicated organizer within these self-governed communities.

A family emergency eventually brought Caleb back to Ann Arbor where, after his experiences in Seattle, he saw the local homeless shelter with new eyes. It was filled beyond capacity, to the point that people had to sleep sitting upright in chairs. At the same time, he began reading articles about the devastating effects of the crashing economy, leading him to realize conditions weren't about to get better any time soon. Caleb had become a strong believer in the self-organized tent cities that he had discovered during his time in Seattle, and he felt there was a chance he might be able to start a similar model in his hometown. "I decided I would start by camping outside by myself," he declared, "and inviting people who didn't have a place to stay to camp with me."

Fast-forward two years later to a humid afternoon in the summer of 2010, when I was dropped off at Camp Take Notice (CTN) with a tent, sleeping bag, my bike, identification, twenty bucks, a couple changes of clothes and some books in my backpack. I hopped the guardrail and headed down a meandering path that led deep into a wooded patch of land carved by a highway interchange. I had visited the camp briefly the previous month as a student, and was now returning for a longer stay as a participating member of the community.

My humble abode while living at Camp Take Notice

The Life of an Unsanctioned Tent City

Over the course of the next month I formed relationships with Caleb and a number of the other campers. Through personal accounts I was able to piece together a full history of the camp between its founding in 2008 and my arrival—allowing me to provide a detailed description of the physical and social organization of each of the six locations that CTN occupied. The intent of the chronicle that follows is to give the reader insight to the character of an informal, unsanctioned tent city, and the resulting interaction with the surrounding urban environment. The context map below illustrates the various locations of CTN, with a more detailed look at each site on the pages that follow. Afterwards, I discuss my personal observations and interactions with the camp.

Ann Arbor Context Map

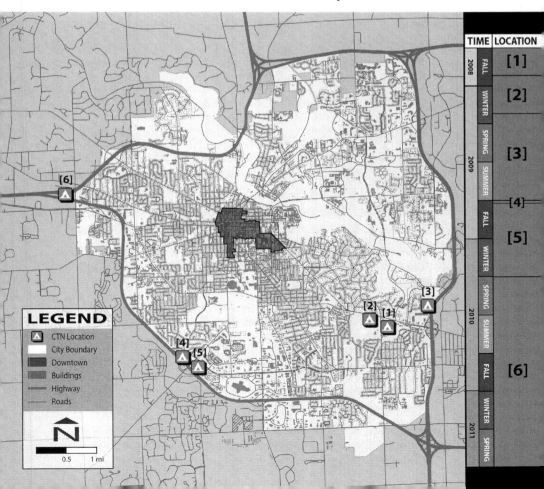

Camp Take Notice
Location 1: Platt Road

Duration: 2 months | Land: Private | Population: 1-4

◊ **Agenda:** Provide shelter

◊ **Site Description:**

A patch of uninhabited woods between some small businesses was chosen as the first site. It was conveniently located next to a bus stop that provided transportation to other parts of the city. The tents were positioned on a low-lying piece of land near the center of the site, which provided dense enough coverage to shield light from within the camp—a fundamental strategy for not attracting outside attention that may lead to an encounter with local authorities. A downside was that the area was prone to flooding. The remains of a demolished building were left from a previous use, and the cap from a large water boiler was adaptively reused for the camp's fire pit.

◊ **Camp Development:**

The first site started with one person and one tent. Incrementally, the camp grew from one to six inhabitants—living in as many as four tents—as Caleb informed others in need about the site. Those who joined the camp were young males who had previously been living on the street.

◊ **Reason for Move:**

The first move was preemptive, following an encounter with city workers who stumbled upon the tents while dragging bags of leaves into the woods. New to the world of illegal camping, Caleb acted with caution and decided to make a move rather than stick around to see what happened.

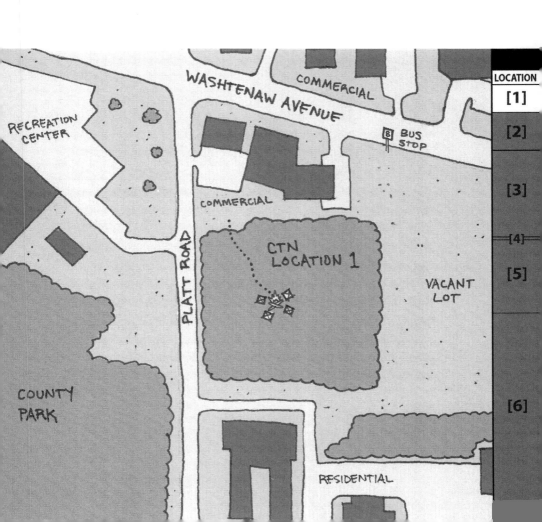

LOCATION

[1]

[2]

[3]

[4]

[5]

[6]

Camp Take Notice
Location 2: Washtenaw Avenue

Duration: 3 months | Land: County | Population: 4-10

◊ **Agenda:** Start a community and build relationships

◊ **Site Description:**

Anticipating the eventuality of relocation, Caleb had already explored alternative sites on foot and while riding the bus. The day following the encounter with city workers, everyone packed up their belongings and crossed the street into County Farm Park. Winter had arrived and the trees had lost their foliage, making it necessary to plunge even deeper into the woods in order to remain undetected from the road. Moving south, an unabridged stream was reached that would act as a natural barrier from the popular recreational walking paths on the other side. It was in this untraveled, densely wooded area that they would settle for a second time. The camp was accessed some distance down the street so that passersby did not see people entering the woods with a direct line to the site. A bus station was again located nearby.

◊ **Camp Development:**

Other members of the camp naturally recognized Caleb as a leader, and an informal community began to emerge. Access to public transportation was on the top of the developing list of criteria for choosing a site. The camp continued to grow in numbers as word on the street spread about the camp, but as the temperature dropped, so did the population as emergency shelter space opened to provide refuge from the harsh winter climate in Michigan. This became a seasonal trend for the camp.

◊ **Reason for Move:**

After three months at the site, the Ann Arbor Police unexpectedly entered the camp and posted an eviction notice, ordering campers to vacate the land within 24 hours. Everyone followed the directive.

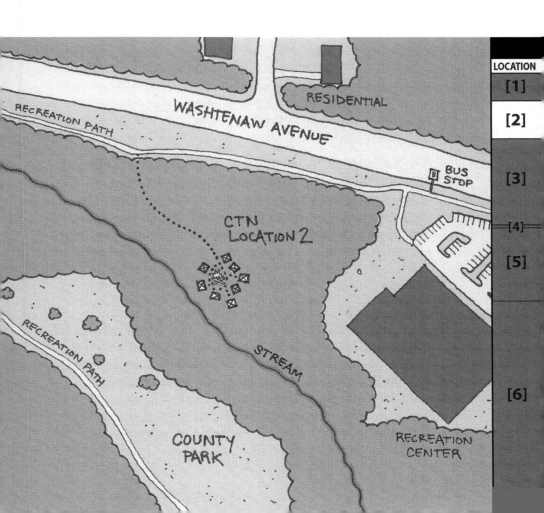

Camp Take Notice
Location 3: Arborland

Duration: 7 months | Land: Private | Population: 4-20

◊ **Agenda:** Organize

◊ **Site Description:**

Following the first formal eviction, the camp relocated behind the Arborland Mall—an area that had a long history of use by the city's homeless. The site was accessed through an existing path behind some big-box stores that led deep into a large wooded patch of land owned by a local developer. Again, the camp was set up far enough back so as to not be in plain sight of the public. The path led much deeper into the woods where remains of previous camps were found, but the group decided to stay close enough to the front to make it more convenient to come and go. Contrary to previous sites, it was assumed that some people would always know the camp was there due to its growing numbers and the resulting foot traffic.

The site was muddy so wooden pallets were brought in to be placed along the paths and underneath the tents—a tactic Caleb had observed during his time at the well-established camps in Seattle. The surrounding shopping center provided a variety of services within walking distance, which allowed for residents to spend a greater amount of time at the camp than at previous locations.

◊ **Camp Development:**

Substantial development occurred within the camp as a result of the convenient location and a longer stay at a single site. The first intentional common space was formed, which consisted of a covered kitchen, a gathering space with two picnic tables inside of a large tent, and a fire pit between these two spaces. The formation of a commons led to improved organization and stronger relationships within the camp. Weekly camp meetings began to be held every Thursday evening. At this time, basic rules were established to regulate stealing, drug use, and other undesirable acts that might jeopardize the stability of the community. It was at this point that the group began to identify as "Camp Take Notice." This marked a distinct turning point for the camp in that they were no longer hiding—the very name invited attention. They became a collective voice unified behind what they believed to be a basic human right: the provision of one's own shelter in the absence of other alternatives.

A partner organization, known as MISSION, was also established to provide political and logistical support to the camp. On Tuesday evenings, meetings began to be held at the public library where the organization would grow to develop a solid base of support for the camp that included both the unhoused and their advocates. The creation of an external support organization marks another criti-

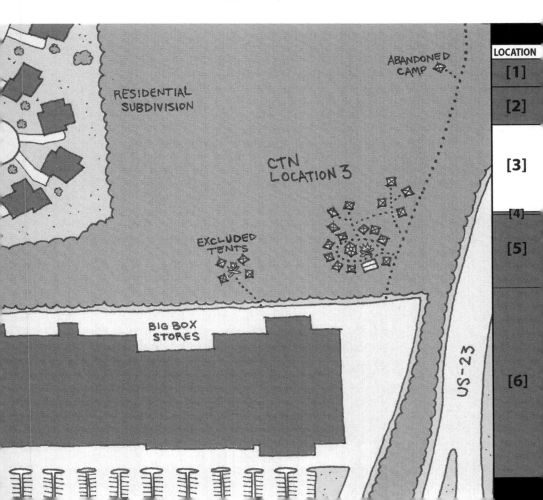

cal step in establishing political recognition—the camp now had an official advocate group in the battle for space. A clear firewall was established between the two entities so as to not interfere with the autonomy of the camp.

A more organized camp meant stricter enforcement of the rules and the development of a judicial process. When a rule was broken, the community began to democratically decide what action was to be taken through a majority vote at the camp meetings. Informal trials were held to determine the fate of problematic campers. But those who were banned from the camp would typically only move a short distance away—often with the assistance of members of CTN and MISSION—forming their own smaller encampment nearby. This physical separation was important in the attempt to establish credibility with formal actors and the larger community.

The population at the Arborland site expanded to as many as twenty residents, which included the addition of females, couples, and pets. The increased traffic to and from the site led to several calls to the police that resulted in a handful of confrontational visits. However, unlike the previous location, a relationship was developed with the police by conversing with them and explaining the group's cause. Caleb even took the initiative to contact the landowner and ask permission to camp there. The owner wouldn't explicitly grant permission, so as to not assume liability risks, but he did agree to not make a complaint at that time.

◊ **Reason for Move:**

After just over half of a year at Arborland, significant physical and organizational development had transpired. But the stay eventually came to an end when the Ann Arbor Police suddenly showed up to evict them. The officers that arrived at the site that day were not the ones that the camp had previously developed relations with. Caleb recalled the officers entering with "angry personalities" and an "obvious agenda." He felt the police must have pressured the landowner into asking for support in evicting them. The police demanded that everyone vacate the property that day.

Camp Take Notice
Location 4: Ann Arbor-Saline Road (West)

Duration: 5 days | Land: State (DOT) | Population: 1-12

◊ **Agenda:** Raise public awareness

◊ **Site Description:**

By this time a pattern of being pushed around by local authorities had become clear. For this reason it was decided to relocate to an unconcealed location where the public could take notice of Camp Take Notice. It was understood that they would not last long at this kind of site, but the strategy was to be in the public spotlight when they were evicted—rather than continuing to be corralled by police without an audience. Caleb informed other campers that they did not have to come, since many were apprehensive about the idea of coming out of hiding, but nearly everyone eventually banded together in support of the plan.

So, after being pushed from the Arborland site, the camp repositioned itself in the center of a highway interchange ramp where they were visible from all angles. Caleb described this site as his "first urban planning experience" since all the tents were set up at once in an organized fashion. Several tents were aligned in a u-shaped layout—even if there was no one actually staying in them—in order to create a spectacle.

> I knew our time at this location was limited and I knew the purpose of the move was political in nature. So, what we tried to do as quickly as possible was lay out the pallets and set up the tents right away because we wanted to be as visible as possible right away. A lot of people fell off pretty quickly as the police started coming out, but I continued putting up the tents anyway to make it look more like a robust community.[65]

The first response was from the Ann Arbor Police after receiving a complaint from a neighboring landowner. The Washtenaw County Police were next to arrive at the scene, and finally the Michigan State Police, after determining it was state land and they had authority. Caleb noted that he took a small amount of pleasure in seeing the police wrestle with the fact that they had evicted a camp the previous day and now it was popping up not too far away the next day. Typically homeless camps are not as organized and commonly disperse after being evicted.

Following the congregation of police departments, two dump trucks from Michigan Department of Transportation (MDOT) arrived as the residents were packing their belongings into bags. While the other campers were willing to leave, Caleb decided that it was time to make a stand. The police told him that they did not understand why he was not cooperating, and that they felt it was a political move with no merit since there were no other campers still present. He responded, "I understand but I have to try," and was then arrested on charges of trespassing and vagrancy.

The next day, as he was being released, he was asked if he was going to repeat the crime, to which he replied, "yes." The man behind the counter told him that he could not release him if he was going to do it again, to which Caleb said "OK," and so they put him back in the holding cell. An hour later they let him go anyway, and he returned to the site to be arrested for a second time only fourteen hours later. All charges were eventually dropped.

◊ **Camp Development:**

This location succeeded in that it brought the issue of homelessness to the attention of the larger community. The local news media reported on the event, just as the group had intended. The articles can be found online—each with a long list of comments. Some readers were very supportive of CTN's efforts with one commenting, "For all the hurdles the homeless have to face, they have organized what seems like a very pleasant community. It is a pity that any time the state sees citizens helping themselves, it begins a campaign of harassment." Others were less supportive replying, "…if you were to watch most of the people in this group for a day, you will see that they are doing little to improve their situation." A popular complaint was that many of the homeless were not from Ann Arbor, and that they have come to the city to exploit its generous services. Still others suggested constructive solutions like scattered site public housing or tenant-run cooperatives. Regardless of the viewpoint, people in Ann Arbor were now taking notice of Camp Take Notice.

◊ **Reason for Move:**

After being released a second time, Caleb was exhausted and realized that the community that had been forming was now dispersing. He considered returning for a third time, but instead decided that it was more imperative to reassemble the camp and continue to organize.

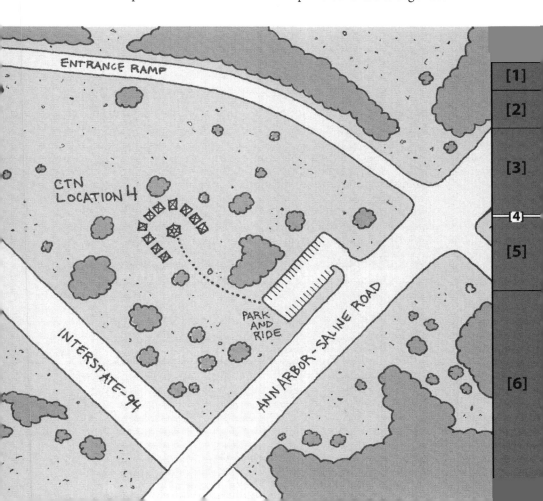

Camp Take Notice

Location 5: Ann Arbor-Saline Road (East)

Duration: 6 months | Land: State (DOT) | Population: 8-22

◊ **Agenda:** Retreat from public visibility and regroup

◊ **Site Description:**

The camp moved to the adjacent highway ramp directly on the other side of the road. This side of road differed in that it was heavily wooded and protected from visibility. The move was simple since people only had to carry their belongings a short distance. It reiterated the point that, if evicted, a tent city will simply reappear somewhere else nearby. The site was also easily accessible by foot and vehicle, which became an increasingly important factor as MISSION members and volunteers began visiting the camp more frequently. An open area that was bounded by trees was chosen, as the campers once again wanted to remain hidden. While the police became immediately aware of CTN's new location they did not take action. Caleb believes the reasons for this were both because they were not in plain sight and because of the immense amount of media attention that resulted from the previous eviction.

Another winter was approaching, but by the third time the veteran campers were better prepared. They had developed solutions for dealing with snow on the top of tents by installing sharply angled tarps. Several blankets and sleeping bags were used, along with small propane heaters that were used inside the tents.

◊ **Camp Development:**

The camp had lost some of its traction and failed to become as cohesive as at the Arborland location. This can be attributed to two reasons. First, cold weather hinders community activity in general. Camp and MISSION meetings continued to be held, but little other communication occurred. Campers took refuge at the local drop-in center and public library, or stuck to their propane-heated tents. Second, relocating twice in a short amount of time took a heavy toll on the organization of the camp. With each move, the community is fragmented to some degree, and requires time to restore a similar sense of cohesion.

◊ **Reason for Move:**

After about six months, MDOT eventually decided to act on the situation. Trespassing signs were posted, resulting in the majority of the community fleeing the site. CTN and MISSION were left with the dilemma of sticking around to make another stand or relocating in advance to avoid further fragmentation. They decided, yet again, to move.

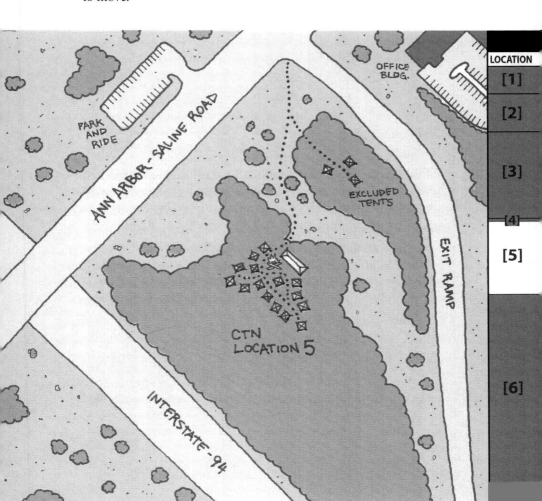

Camp Take Notice
Location 6: Wagner Road

Duration: 2+ years | Land: Sate (DOT) | Population: 20-70

◊ **Agenda:** Find sanctioned land

◊ **Site Description:**

Using an emergency fund set aside by MISSION, a moving truck was rented to move the community to a new site—this time just outside of city limits in Scio Township. The site was once again on MDOT land, and included nine-acres of leftover space created by the junction of two highways. Similar to the Arborland site, the land had long been inhabited by the homeless. In fact, CTN was actually invited to the site by an individual who had been camping there alone for a few months. Upon moving to the site, CTN and MISSION cleared out several truckloads of garbage that had accumulated over the years both from previous camps and illegal commercial dumping.

The site was spacious, concealed, and well-defined on all sides. While highway traffic made for a noisy environment, the community was able to spread out uninterruptedly more than at any previous location. One resident described it as an "off-the-grid sanctuary surrounded by the grid." A meandering path from Wagner Road led a quarter mile into the woods to a clearing created by towering pines. Here, the community gathering and cooking areas were established. From there, a number of diverging paths were formed, each leading to a different pocket of tents. The path network expanded organically, and more advanced features were developed as the camp continued to grow over time.

A bus stop was again conveniently located adjacent to the camp entrance. Restrooms were used at the gas station and bowling alley down the street, and campers were able to fill up large jugs of water at a nearby car dealership. Garbage was collected at a specified location near the road, and a volunteer would pick it up and dispose of it each week. Most campers would take the bus, bike, or walk the three miles to downtown each day, and some would often not return to camp until the last outgoing bus.

◊ **Camp Development:**

With another long stay at a single location, CTN was able to re-establish the level of community that had transpired at the Arborland site. The development of an "executive committee" was a critical advancement for better regulating the rules of a larger camp. Elections for this position began to be held every three months. At this time, campers nominated others in the community, and a democratic vote was held to fill the four positions. Their role was to maintain peace and order in the day-to-day operation of the camp—until the village

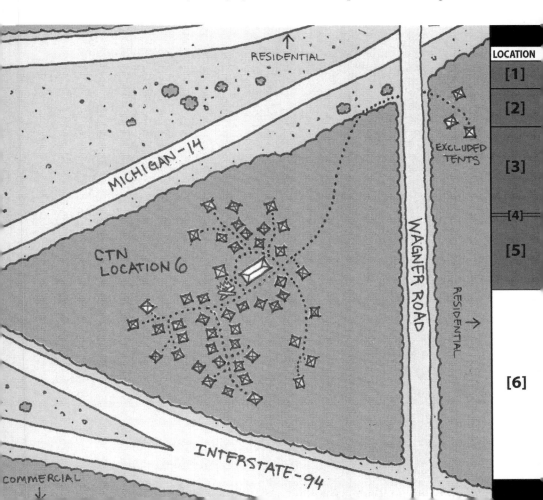

as a whole could make final decisions at the weekly meeting. As one committee member put it, their goal was "to provide a safe place for people to lay their heads and to keep the blue lights away." With a majority vote, the executive committee had the power to evict someone who committed a serious offense. The eviction could then be appealed to a camp meeting, where each member of the community had the chance to vote after hearing testimony from both sides.

At this location MISSION received 501(c)3 status. A "sanctioned land search committee" was formed in order to identify and pursue potential legal sites to which the camp could move, and more formal conversations ensued. "Safety committee" meetings began to be held, which included representatives from MDOT and the county and state police departments (the City of Ann Arbor did not partake in these discussions since the camp was now across the street from the city line). At the meetings, these entities were updated on the current conditions of the camp and the status of the land search committee. In short, they wanted to see that progress towards a viable alternative was being actively pursued, and did not want to see the camp remain stagnant. MDOT, who owned the land CTN was located on, stated that they would not seek eviction as long as the camp did not become a liability or attract public complaints.

Covered sitting area outside of someone's tent

Findings

In the summer of 2010, I spent one month living at the Wagner Road site. Here, I was able to participate in the day-to-day life of a self-organized, unsanctioned tent city. The experience and close relationships I formed with several of my new neighbors strongly influenced my early perspectives on this subject. Every other portrayal I had encountered—whether it was sympathetic or antagonistic—had cast the American tent city in a shameful light. The sympathetic would place blame on the failures of the larger community while the antagonistic placed blame on the campers. However, through observing and interacting within the camp, I found qualities that positively address many of the shortfalls we find in traditional responses to homelessness, and housing in general. For example, consider the following dynamics, which I found to be the defining characteristics of CTN.

A Place To Be

While there is widespread criticism of the substandard conditions, few give credit to the fact that the camp is consistently providing a much-needed service by offering emergency shelter to a population with no other place to go. The living situation may be far from ideal by conventional standards, but at the very least, camp is a place to call home. I found this to have a profoundly positive impact on an individual's outlook on life. Caleb often referred to this as the "sense of agency" that results from having a place to be—as small and meager as it may be:

> Having lost power over the direction of your life, when you are in a tent community and you take control of your own little square footage of space—your own tent—you have an area that is yours and you have ways that you can interact in the community where your voice and your opinions have impact. And so that takes people away from the position of being on the receiving end...[66]

The tent community provides a unique opportunity in that it allows those experiencing homelessness to invest value in space and to create a place of one's own. With time, those staying at CTN gradu-ally improved and personalized the areas around their tent by adding awnings, decks, fences, shelving, and personal cooking areas. Having a place of one's own re-establishes a sense of ownership and responsibil-ity—an experience that can better position those trying to reintegrate themselves into society.

There is a plethora of research that demonstrates the negative effects of some *not* having a stable place to be, both on the individ-ual and the larger community. Homeless shelters aim to mitigate the impact, but fall short in capacity, and in the process strip their clients of dignity by failing to respect privacy and autonomy. People are sepa-rated from their spouses and pets, and either lack a place to store their belongings or have limited access to them if they do have storage. Dani-elle, a resident at CTN, described her experience in a self-organized tent city in comparison to staying at the local shelter:

> I find this [tent city] better than the shelter. At the shelter you're required to get up at 6:30 in the morning. Wake up! Be gone by 7:30 and you have to take all your stuff with you for the entire day. If you're a resident you can't get back to the residential floor until 5:00pm. So you're left carrying around all this stuff, which is detri-mental to trying to find work. At least out here [tent city] you have your own place you can set your stuff down, come and get it as you need. It's actually a much more prime example for someone who's actually trying to find work, trying to do something. Because you can get up in the morning, do whatever you need to, change into dress clothes for your interview, go to the job interview, then you come back here and change so you're not dirtying up those clothes for your interviews.[67]

During my stay at CTN, Danielle ran for a county commissioner position, enrolled at a community college, and eventually transitioned to an apartment. The value of simply having a place to be may be taken for granted by most, but it is a critical first step for anyone trying to improve their situation. A self-organized tent community can provide a place to plant that step when all else fades away.

Horizontal Organization and Mutual Aid

In the traditional homeless shelter system a vertical, top-down management approach is taken. A staff is employed to provide services for the clients (the homeless). The help comes from above and people are not left with much to give to their neighbor. There is typically a rigid set of rules that determine who can receive the service, at what time, and for how long. A common complaint by those at CTN who had previously stayed at the local shelter was that it left them with no time to do anything else. It is easy to become consumed by the inflexible routine of these services, creating a culture of dependence that makes it difficult to ever transition out of. This formal structure not only alienates the client, but also requires sizeable public funding to develop and operate.

The self-organized tent city exemplifies an alternative approach based on horizontal organization—where people in a similar situation work together to improve their collective standard of living. Tate, a military veteran at the camp described this as "camaraderie"—stating, "The camp provides a needed alternative to shelters... to get yourself back on your feet with the support network that we've established here. A homeless person will tend to be segregated and withdrawn—we have to re-engage those social skills."

Unlike vertical organization, the horizontal alternative appeals to a broad population. Through Caleb's experiences as a tent city organizer in Seattle, he found that one of people's strongest desires is not to receive, but to be a provider. He emphasized: "The ability to have something to give laterally to your friends next to you is something that is very healing for people." This dynamic of reciprocity within the self-organized tent city, like many of these findings, is something that can be liberating to all members of society, not just the unhoused.

Powerful

Self-Governance

Horizontal organization encourages residents of a politically organized tent community to engage in the act of direct democracy, creating a decision-making system in which all members of the group have equal voice. At CTN, this was practiced through regular weekly camp meetings. During this time, residents had the opportunity to form camp rules, evict members who broke rules, and elect an executive committee to maintain order on a day-to-day basis. While there was little commitment required from those who lived at CTN, it was emphasized that everyone must attend the weekly meeting.

Evicting someone from camp was an action not taken lightly by the community. Some refused to ever vote someone out no matter what the circumstance. As one resident described, "This [living at CTN] is the lowest rung on the ladder, and kicking someone off of that just doesn't seem right." However, the majority of residents felt it was a necessary act, since failing to do so could jeopardize the existence of the camp. At first this meant they only enforced temporary bans from the camp, but eventually evolved to include permanent evictions. This served a dual purpose: it protected the quality of life within the camp and also improved the group's credibility in the larger community. Through trial and error, a more sophisticated and better defined process for governance unfolded over time.

In the United States, our governing process has become so intricate and specialized that the intimate act of self-governance is unknown to most. We are left to pick between two candidates—the one on the left or the one on the right—to represent and make decisions for us, leaving many apathetic. CTN practiced a more direct form of democracy that is foreign to the average American citizen. This was another factor that contributed to the "sense of agency" described by Caleb. In combining a place to be with the opportunity to practice self-governance, the tent community creates an empowering environment for the unhoused, who are often otherwise left dispirited. People who had become accustomed to being unheard and forgotten were now making decisions that directly impacted the community in which they lived. The homeless had become advocates.

Community and Collaboration

When one is unhoused, the advantages to living in community are tremendous. There is extensive literature on the culture and social organization among the impoverished in general, but the politically organized tent city promotes a distinct emphasis on community building. The conjunction of a place to be, horizontal organization, and self-governance creates what many residents at CTN described as a "sense of belonging"—making this a model for collaboration.

This dynamic became clear to me within the first hour I arrived at the informal camp beside the highway. Winding down the wooded path on a summer afternoon, I came to a clearing created by towering pines. The path split in various directions leading to separate pockets of tents, each of which appeared to be empty. I began searching for an open space to set up my tent, but without much luck—that is until someone emerged from a nearby tent and introduced himself as Nick. There were no cleared spots available so he brought out a rake and shovel to help me clear a modest space near his, and we spent the next hour erecting my temporary home. He told me that whenever a new person arrives, whoever is around at the time usually helps them to find a spot and make sure their basic needs are met. I had not brought a pillow so Nick insisted that I take one of his.

Another example of the strong presence of community and collaboration at camp came at the lowest point during my stay. As usual, I started the day by walking my bike up the trail and over the guardrail. Hopping on I began to ride over the highway. A large truck approaching from behind caused me to swerve out of the way—my bike scraped the side of a high curb, but I was able to maintain balance as the truck sped by. I looked down to find my bike's chain dragging on the pavement. My knowledge of bikes was novice at best, but I could tell the damage was serious. The metal piece near the rear wheel that held the chain in place was cracked in half. Having only a few bucks left at the time, I faced the fact that I would probably not be able to get it fixed.

This may not seem so devastating to most, but a bike is an invaluable possession to someone in this type of situation. Being able to get downtown each day is imperative for campers to get food, showers, and services—and to just get away from the drama that can build at camp. While the site was conveniently located directly next to a bus line, I could not afford the fare out and back each day. I realized I would have to walk the three miles to downtown most of the time, which took about an hour. Pissed off, I chained my bike to the nearest road sign and got on an incoming bus since I had a meeting to get to for the camp's non-profit organization. I paid the $1.50 fare and took a seat in the back where I could dwell on my plight.

After getting some dinner at the local shelter, I decided to walk back to camp instead of spending the last of my money on the bus. I passed my dejected bike along the way and began to push it back towards camp. As I entered, someone asked me how my day was, and I explained what had happened. As we examined the bike near the community's gathering area, others joined us, including Dave who identified the broken piece as a rear derailleur. He began telling stories of how he had worked for years fixing bikes. While typically reserved around me, Dave became quite engaged with the chance to help with a problem he was knowledgeable about. A number of old bikes were lying around so he suggested we replace my derailleur with one from an unused bike—a task for which we needed a particular tool. We sought out Tate, the military veteran with a wide selection of tools. Tate sifted through a large case to find the right fit. We were able to easily remove the broken piece, and then began trying to replace it with the unused derailleurs. After some time, we found that none of them fit my bike properly. I was still out of luck.

The next day I met with Caleb who, upon hearing my problem, helped me get a "Fare Deal" card that reduced my bus fare to $0.75. Panhandling a few quarters from time to time or turning in a few bottles for the deposit was not a problem (ten cents each in Michigan!). Although my bike was still busted, I felt better about the situation knowing there was a network of friends ready to help when needed. It also reaffirmed my belief in the positive personal and social dynamics of the self-organized tent city. At CTN, individuals facing similar hardship were working collectively while simultaneously creating opportunities for personal healing and growth. In this scenario, the person with the problem becomes a vital part of the solution—a critical component to preserve in developing a model forward.

Safety

A direct benefit of living in a tight-knit community is the resulting sense of safety. This asset is particularly important for the unhoused, who face a great deal of vulnerability to violence due to the insecurity of their living spaces. In 2009 alone, a report by the National Coalition for the Homeless lists 43 homeless individuals who died as a result of violent attacks, and a total of 291 such deaths have occurred since the attacks began to be recorded in 1991. Included were instances of people being beaten, raped, and even set on fire simply because they were homeless. The same report found that violent attacks on the homeless are now greater than all other categories of hate crimes combined.[68]

Security was a primary benefit of living in a tent community cited by members of CTN. People often spoke of looking out for one another and pulling together in tough times. As one camper put it, "If you start trouble with one of us, you start trouble with all of us." He described how he felt safe knowing that—if an outsider were to walk into camp in the middle of the night—there would be at least twenty others within shouting distance that would have his back. I shared this feeling of security during my stay at CTN, often feeling safer there than at my single-apartment back in Cincinnati.

Diverse Population

Who are these people that live in America's tent cities? At CTN they were men and women who ranged from late teens to early sixties—White, Black, Asian, and Latino; veterans, bohemians, unemployed, employed, college graduates, and one even with a masters degree. Many dealt with one or more physical or mental impairments.

Why were they living in a tent city? The number of reasons were as abundant as the number of people living there. Each story was unique. Going into it I expected to hear accounts of unemployment and foreclosures caused by the recession, but the longer I stayed at CTN the more I realized that this was not the case. Most people had a history of going in and out of housing periodically—regardless of economic conditions—often due to an inability to find and maintain long-term employment. For some, this was their first experience being homeless, and they preferred the do-it-yourself nature of the self-organized tent city—taking an independent approach to getting back on their feet, rather than facing the humiliation of entering the local shelter system.

I found that the housed population has an overwhelmingly misguided perception of the people living in tent cities. This is likely a result of how the average person encounters homelessness. The chronically homeless in the poorest state of mental and physical capacity are often the most visible and therefore shape a generalized understanding of a larger population. The stereotypical "homeless man" that most envision was not who was living at CTN. As a result of camp rules and the self-governing process, these individuals did not last long in an organized environment. In fact, the average eye would likely not even register many of the people who resided at CTN as "homeless" if they passed them on the sidewalk or sat next to them on the bus.

Strategic Siting

As the camp continued to relocate, the list of desirable site characteristics became more extensive and better defined. In talking with some of the long-time members of CTN, I became more aware of important aspects to take into consideration when choosing a site for an unsanctioned tent city. The most crucial of which included:

◊ Avoid private land: While this is not always the case, private landowners often become hostile towards the tent city as soon as they discover its existence, and local authorities are then likely to act quicker in dismantling it. Instead, choosing underutilized public land places the tent city in more of a grey area. If the camp is politically organized, it puts authorities in a tough situation, and the camp is likely to exist for a longer duration.

◊ Avoid public view: The site must be out of the direct view of the public or else chances of a quick eviction are high. A prime example of this can be seen in the drastically differing results for CTN at location 4 versus 5. Location 4 was in plain sight and local authorities took action immediately. However, after moving directly across the street, the camp existed for six months before being evicted, even though authorities were aware of their presence. The primary difference was that the latter provided dense coverage from public view. This is why wooded areas are commonly chosen, unless a camp is trying to make a political statement.

◊ Locate close to transportation: Locating in close proximity to public transportation is critical since campers rarely have access to cars. Even bus fare is sometimes inaccessible, so being within reasonable walking and biking distance to the downtown is also important. When members are stranded without transportation in this kind of an environment, it can be harmful to morale. A primary goal in choosing the sites for CTN was to strategically locate out of sight yet still accessible to public transportation.

◊ Locate close to services: The unsanctioned tent city lacks on-site access to water, garbage collection, and toilets. As a result, proximity to services like convenience stores and gas stations becomes imperative to the health and sanitation of the camp. Access to social services, which are mostly located downtown, is also necessary to help campers improve their situation. Libraries are another key public service where the unhoused can access technology, information, and a place to be.

Organic Growth

The informal development of a tent city stands in stark contrast to the grid pattern found elsewhere in the city. Rather than being formally planned in advance, they grow and evolve organically. This does not necessarily mean, however, that they are unplanned. "It is a misunderstanding to say that only dominated militaristic or modern cultures and geometric cities are planned," argues neighborhood activist Mark Lakeman. "What distinguishes early settlement forms from later ones is more a question of who is doing the planning and how much freedom is left to the people."[69] This was certainly the case at CTN, where the residents themselves were free to plan their personal and common spaces.

With time, more people set up camp, and each addition became a reaction to the existing environment. The orientation and spacing of each tent was determined by the inhabitants desire for privacy versus security. Jane Jacobs' theory that more "eyes upon the street" results in safer environments was evident as many chose to camp in clusters.[70] Tarps were erected to stay dry, fences were built to create edge, and decks were built for leisure. Common areas also evolved significantly as more materials, both salvaged and donated, accumulated at the camp.

Christopher Alexander describes this type of organic growth in great detail. With a focus on the idea of "growing whole," he offers seven rules for developing organically in which "every increment of construction must be made in such a way as to heal the city."[71] This process is evident in informal tent cities and shantytowns not necessarily because the inhabitants know these rules, but because this is the "natural way of building." The result is a feeling of authenticity—or what Alexander describes as environments that are "alive"—that is unmatched by the "staged images" of formal development described by Groth and Corjin.

While not as complex as the shantytowns of Third World countries, the American tent city still demonstrates organic growth. The lack of complexity is not so much the result of a reduced necessity as much as it is the continual disruption of this type of development by formal actors. As described in Chapter 2, just as members of tent cities shape space to fit their needs, formal actors are continually re-controlling those spaces according to their own designs. The chronicle of CTN demonstrates

Fence made from branches to define a single entrance to the tent

how moving a camp can take a significant toll on its organization and physical development. Many campers were apprehensive about getting too comfortable because, as they would often say, "we might not be here tomorrow." It was not until the most recent site that enough stability was achieved to warrant substantial growth. But quite possibly the best U.S. example may be "Tent City" in Nashville, which I will turn to in the next case study. This camp remained in the same location for nearly three decades without regulation, and gradually expanded to over one hundred tents and makeshift structures.

Eviction

After more than two years at the Wagner Road site, the camp was evicted from the site on June 22, 2012. With a population of around 70 people at the time, CTN was given three weeks notice by MDOT to vacate the land or face possible arrest on trespassing charges. In the end, the eviction was prompted by NIMBY opposition.

The camp had conducted outreach in the surrounding neighborhood and many neighbors supported the camp, saying that the area had been less troublesome with CTN there when compared to the previous clandestine camps in the past. But one neighbor, more vocal than the

A tent tucked into the woods with covered cooking area in front

rest, collected over one-hundred signatures on a petition to have the camp evicted.[72] MDOT then decided to re-evaluate its neutral position on the camp following the public complaint and also because the camp's population was growing. Two days prior to the eviction, authorities began erecting an eight foot tall chain-link fence to block the nine acres of land—"to resolve the issue once and for all." The regional manager of MDOT noted that there were concerns that the fence may be unsightly, but "keeping the homeless out is of greater concern."[73]

In conjunction with the eviction notice, the Michigan State Housing Development Authority announced that 40 one-year housing subsidies would be made available for some of the campers. However, this did not necessarily guarantee shelter. The subsidies require renting from a private landlord and an inspection of the property. Landlords are under no obligation to rent to someone with a subsidy, and in a college town, students (with a parent's co-signature) are typically more attractive to lease to.

More than a month after the eviction, less than half of the 40 subsidies had helped former CTN campers move into apartments. A further attempt to minimize the impact of the eviction was to open 50 temporary spaces at the local shelter specifically to accommodate the CTN population. However, this only consisted of floor space in the basement—with just three feet of space between people—and no place to store personal belongings. Only a few of the campers took this route following the eviction.[74]

While some were optimistic that the subsidies would give them the chance they needed to re-enter society, others spoke of missing the sense of "belonging" and "family" that they no longer had. Many felt that the subsidies were only a temporary solution, and argued that the money could have been better spent. CTN was an unofficial program, but it offered a very important service not being offered anywhere else in the city. In fact, while they are unlikely to formally admit it, the local shelter, hospital, and police routinely sent people with nowhere else to go to the camp. There, this destitute population was compassionately welcomed and provided with a place to be, provided they did not persistently disrupt the community.

At the Wagner site alone, the camp served hundreds of people on a shoestring budget funded largely by the local faith-based community. Instead of looking to improve this citizen-driven initiative that was addressing the needs of a diverse population, large sums of tax dollars were spent on erecting a fence and short-term subsidies with an estimated cost of around half a million dollars.

How could this money have been spent more effectively? How can cities respond to what they perceive as intractable homeless camps with long-term solutions rather than temporary fixes? And how can the positive dynamics of these informal programs be retained in developing a formal solution? Several more case studies will be covered next to see how other cities are handling a similar situation in an effort to better answer these questions.

Following the eviction, an anonymous donation allowed MISSION to purchase a house on a three acre property. In the tradition of Dorothy Day and Jane Addams, it is being utilized as a "House of Hospitality" for those experiencing homelessness. CTN and MISSION continue to hold weekly meetings at the house, and while they are regularly attended, the members are now dispersed throughout the area. However, they are now pursuing a planned unit development to add a tent and micro-housing community in the back of the property. Known as Homeward Bound, the project aims to re-establish the first rung on the ladder out of homelessness.

Chapter 6

Nashville's Organic Camp

• • •

**What does a complete lack of formal infrastructure
and organization look like?**

In early May 2010, a massive flood resulted in the evacuation of Nashville's long-standing "Tent City." Despite several attempts to shut down the camp, the settlement had survived on the same five acres of land since the mid-1980s. During this time, many residents of Tent City moved from tents to makeshift shelters built from whatever materials were available—namely tarps, rope, pallets, and reclaimed lumber. A site inventory showed that there were roughly 140 tents or structures at one point. But in the end, it was natural disaster rather than formal eviction that caused the eventual exodus from under the highway bridge near Hermitage Avenue. More than 100 people were displaced from the camp, and then later informed by local authorities that they could not return to their makeshift homes due to contamination caused by the flood. In this chapter, I examine the product of completely unregulated development, and the subsequent efforts for formal recognition.

An Informal Relic

Three months after the flood, I visited the abandoned site to see what remained of the camp. Starting down a dirt path into the woods, I

A makeshift home, basketball hoop, and scattered 40 oz. bottles after the flood

Gate installed in fence to divide enclaves within the camp

Wood-burning stove and personal possessions inside of makeshift home

soon crossed a railroad track with highway bridges looming hundreds of feet overhead. It felt as though I was entering a lost civilization. What was once a bustling sanctuary for those who did not fit the mold of conventional society had now been left eerily deserted. The ruins of the makeshift homes were all that remained—tarps, pallets, and scattered refuse littered the landscape. Taking a look inside some of the more intricate shelters that were still standing, I found wood stoves, mattresses, curtains, carpeting, and shelving with canned food and various personal possessions. The remains were a testament of the ingenuity of the people who once called it home.

It was clear that the camp grew organically over time as more of the city's marginalized came to take refuge at Tent City. Gates were installed in existing fences, dividing the informal settlement into separate enclaves. Even after the disaster, I was able to distinguish various neighborhoods within the camp that possessed characteristics specific to the residents that once lived there. For example, in the far back of the site near the river, there was a basketball hoop and the landscape was littered with 40 ounce beer bottles that had been dispersed by the flood. It appeared to be where the long-time residents had gathered, piecing together elaborate shanties on the banks of the Cumberland River as materials became available. There was also a less defined area near the front and closer to the railroad tracks that was far less developed. Here, I found clusters of basic tents with few possessions, which appeared to have been settled by newer inhabitants. Other clusters of tents and shelters existed in zones between these two extremes.

Standing in what was once the center of this informal community, it became clear why the camp was able to endure for nearly three decades. The five acres of public land was the epitome of residual space. Bound between railroad tracks to the east and the Cumberland River to the west, the site was scattered with concrete pillars rising hundreds of feet to support the speeding interstate highway traffic overhead (pictured on cover). It was out of sight and out of mind—there were no neighbors to upset. At the time of my visit, nature was already beginning to reclaim the abandoned camp. Local authorities had claimed the site to be contaminated and uninhabitable, and I was told that the police began to monitor the site to ensure that no one returned.

The Backstory

Shortly thereafter, I met with Doug Sanders at the Amos House—a Catholic Worker house providing supportive housing to a few of the one-time residents of Tent City. Sanders—a minister and a primary proponent of the camp—provided me with first hand insight on the organization and development of Tent City prior to the flood.

For a number of years, the site was a well-kept secret, remaining a small-scale sanctuary for a select few living completely off the grid. But with time, word spread and more of the city's marginalized began to settle there, expanding to whatever boundaries they could without any formal structure or supervision. There were a few instances where the camp had sprawled onto adjacent private land in which case they were eventually forced to retreat. With no municipal infrastructure or support, the camp quickly began to accumulate mounds of garbage and debris. At this point, it was largely a community of people simply living next to each other with no place else to go. While some level of organization occurred among the different enclaves within the camp, there were no overarching community agreements or rules.

Then, on the verge of being shutdown in 2007, a coalition of faith-based communities stepped in to clean up the camp, and began facilitating better communication and organization within the informal community. Sanders, who was among this group, described his initial impressions of the camp as "unstructured, unsupervised, and unplanned." But he also witnessed a positive side to the camp—where people were "building something out of nothing"—and he felt it could be restructured and revived.

> Tent City, in my opinion, is nothing more than a desperate cry for community, as dysfunctional as it is. It's a need that is being addressed outside of the system in many ways... The opportunity is to say, can we embrace that and include it in a way that it actually becomes a part of the larger community rather than being pushed off to the side?[75]

Sanders felt that the support from the faith-based community resulted in a safer and healthier Tent City. Monthly meetings began to be held, loose rules were formed, and some residents began to take on responsibility for maintaining a more orderly camp. But the land was owned by the state's department of transportation and existed on a floodplain. At one point, the highway bridges that stood above the camp were in need of renovation, and the city announced that the camp would have to be removed by the time that construction was set to begin. But in May 2010, ten feet of water filled the floodplain, the site was evacuated, and the community was displaced.

Following the natural disaster, Tent City was relocated about ten miles away on two acres of a 120 acre site in Antioch. The land, owned by a local businessman, was practically in the middle of nowhere, yet the tent city still faced immediate NIMBY opposition. Neighboring residents demanded a city inspection of the site, and the informal use was found to be in violation of zoning regulations. The tent city refugees that had gathered there were given thirty days to clear the land, and they soon scattered into smaller camps throughout the city.

"Save Tent City"

Tent City no longer exists in Nashville, or at least not in the unified fashion that it once did. Following the evacuation, some residents received short-term housing vouchers while others were left on their own to find a new place to camp. Sanders and others continued to lead a "Save Tent City" campaign, and Nashville's Homeless Commission was directed to meet over the course of a 90 day period to form a proposal for a sanctioned tent city. The commission included members from public, private, religious, and non-profit sectors—and there was also a special election held to add one homeless representative to the commission.

After my visit to the deserted site, I headed to a park adjacent to the public library where the election was being held. Four of the former residents from the original Tent City had been nominated. By the time I had arrived, a mass of Nashville's homeless population had already gathered there. It turned out that a film crew was also in attendance, filming a documentary for the Oprah Winfrey Network—presumably a follow up to the Sacramento tent city story from 2009.

After talking with a few people, I discovered the reason that many of them were there was because of word that there would be free food at the event. The film crew had arranged for food carts to be brought in that gave away free hot dogs and snow cones to those who showed up for the election. After all, the scene in the documentary would not be very impressive without a crowd. I learned that they had been documenting the story since before the flood, and as they continued to dictate the event, the election suddenly seemed like an elaborate scheme to stage an interesting conclusion to their documentary. Nominees were placed in front of cameras to debate, and others were instructed to circle around so the cameras could catch the drama. At one point, I was even asked to move because I was taking photographs in the line of where the crew was trying to shoot.

Who won the election you might ask? My response: Why should there even be an election in the first place? Why shouldn't all four candidates get a say in the future of their living space? Why not more? A key principle of community planning is to include the people you are planning for in the process, but it appears the formal commission never considered what they were planning to be a community. The documentary that was being filmed, *Tent City USA*, covers the brief remainder of the story.

It turned out that Nashville's Mayor still had to approve the new seat on the commission—a process that took several months to even receive a response. When the elected representative finally got a chance to attend the meetings, others politely listened, but nothing came of it. The film concludes that the commission's efforts to sanction a tent city were unsuccessful, and that Tent City remains scattered in dozens of smaller encampments. However, it appears that the consideration by Nashville's formal actors was merely a staged image, and the idea of a legal tent city was never sincerely given a chance. In the next case study we will move to Seattle, which provides precedent for more genuine interaction between informal and formal actors to achieve a sanctioned tent city that works for both sides.

Chapter 7

Seattle's Itinerant Camp

• • •

**How can a community creatively adapt to
moving every three months?**

The history of Seattle's push for a sanctioned tent city can be
traced back to 1990, when a group of 25 homeless individuals decided
to establish a self-managed camp near the Seattle Center. Known as
"Tent City," the camp provided a relatively safe environment for those
without shelter through a code of conduct based on sobriety, non-violence, cooperation, and participation.[76] While the city already had an
extensive history of homeless encampments, this marked the beginning of the most organized effort.[77] The campaign was led by SHARE, a
grassroots organization of around 100 homeless or previously homeless
individuals. This initial camp was eventually disbanded, but only after
the establishment of an indoor, transitional housing program that would
also be self-managed, known as the Aloha Inn. Since then, SHARE has
evolved into SHARE/WHEEL—an organization of over 500 members,
and the largest shelter provider in King County. Their network includes
15 indoor shelters and 2 tent cities. However, the organization distinguishes itself from a social service organization and instead identifies as
a "self-help group." This chapter looks at how this has allowed SHARE/
WHEEL to serve a large population with such few resources, specifically through their venerable tent city model.

A row of tents at Tent City 3 in a church parking lot

A group tent with beds made from milk crates

Portable toilets with camp rules posted

Sanctioning a Tent City

Following the break up of the first Tent City, the next endeavor—known as Tent City 2—was formed on public land in 1998, but the camp was literally bulldozed within a short amount of time. Then, in 2000, the group resurrected as Tent City 3 on private land. Due to a violation of land use code, the camp was forced to relocate—an act that would be required of the group several times over the course of the next two years.

But by 2002, an agreement was finally reached with the city through a consent decree in *SHARE/WHEEL and El Centro de la Raza v. the City of Seattle et al.* (El Centro was the non-profit organization hosting the tent city at the time). It was noted that, despite an increase in city expenditures for emergency shelters, the city was still unable to shelter over 1,000 citizens. The agreement allowed for one tent city, managed by SHARE/WHEEL, to be sanctioned on private or public land within the city, provided that it followed a specific process and list of conditions. This included forming an agreement with the host property owner, a maximum capacity of 100 residents, no children, strict enforcement of a code of conduct, a 20 foot buffer or view obscuring fence, and providing proper notice to the surrounding community. Of the conditions set, the most cumbersome was that the tent city would have to relocate to a new site every three months. Under the agreement, Tent City 3 could stay at the same site twice over a two year period provided that the stays were non-consecutive.[78]

Following this ruling, Tent City 4 was formed in 2004. While Tent City 3 continued to rotate among sites within city limits, its successor sprung up in Seattle's adjacent suburbs in the Eastside. The camp first appeared in the town of Bothell, where no current ordinance existed for homeless encampments. As the town began to move forward with an eviction, a church invited the refugees to use their property. Here, the camp claimed protection under the Religious Land Use and Institutionalized Persons Act (RLUIPA). This federal law allows religious institutions to bypass zoning regulations that may burden the free exercise of religion. Since then—following the acquisition of a special use permit—a network of religious institutions throughout King County have hosted the camp on their property for three months at a time.

This approach was further formalized in 2009. Washington State Law House Bill 1956 now guarantees the right of religious institutions throughout the state of Washington to host temporary encampments on their property. The court found that denying this right would place a substantial burden on the free exercise of religion, and prohibited local governments from imposing excessive fees, liability insurance requirements, or any special conditions other than to protect public health and safety.

While SHARE/WHEEL is the non-profit organization that is formally recognized as managing Tent City 3 and 4, both camps maintain a strong democratic system of self-governance. Each is limited to a maximum of 100 members, and each is typically at full capacity. With such a large population, an "executive committee" is elected to serve as representatives for the group as a whole. A "tent-coordinator" from SHARE/WHEEL serves as a liaison between the tent city and the site host. To be admitted, one must pass a background screening (no outstanding warrants or sex offense convictions) and agree to the camp's code of conduct, which is based on the principles of sobriety, non-violence, cooperation, and participation established by the original Tent City.

A Tour of Tent City 3

It's 2011 when I take a tour of Tent City 3 in the parking lot of St. Joseph's Church—administered by Carole, a resident who is on duty to provide this service. There was no need to schedule a visit, though a resident must accompany visitors at all times. Upon entering the camp through the single opening in the makeshift fence, someone in a bright orange vest requires that I sign in. The vest designates that he is on security duty—a 24 hour service provided by the residents themselves, with each person being required to serve two shifts per weeks.

Carole introduces me to Eric. He serves on the executive committee, which means that his primary role is to enforce the camp's code of conduct. Eric rummages through the administrative tent to proudly hand me four pages of "barrable offenses." Each offense is followed by a corresponding penalty, which ranges from extra security shifts to being required to leave the camp for a specified period of time (referred to as a bar). Running, riding a bike, or spitting in camp can result in two additional security shifts. Missing a security shift results in a three day bar from the camp. Residents can be permanently barred for more serious offenses like theft, harassment, or being the cause of a non-medical 911 call. "Being smelly" can result in a warning for the first offense and a three day bar for the next occurrence.

Some of the rules, such as this last one, may seem overly strict, but Carole reminds me that the residents themselves have voted to adopt each of them based upon experience. Similar to CTN, one of the requirements of being a resident is attending weekly meetings (an unexcused absence here is a three day bar). If a common nuisance bothers enough people, they can make it a barrable offense, with the intent of creating a higher quality of life within the camp.

Because a visual barrier is required per the agreement with the city—and due to the temporary nature of each stay—a moveable, makeshift fence has been concocted out of tarps, 2x4s, and milk crates filled with rocks. These materials—along with pallets, rope, and duct tape—are utilized throughout the camp for a variety of DIY solutions. Tent City 3 exemplifies resourcefulness while maintaining a tidy aesthetic.

All residents are required to earn a certain number of "community credits" by completing various operational and maintenance activities, and some have adopted designated roles within the camp. Patrick, whom I meet under the community tent, tells me about his role as "move master" as he sits at a table playing another resident in a game of chess. As soon as the camp moves to a new site they begin looking for the next location. Once a host is confirmed, Patrick prints out an aerial map of the site using Google Maps. He uses this to plan the move and to sketch out a conceptual layout for the next camp. All existing residents are required to help with the move or else they are not allowed to stay at the next site.

At the site I'm visiting, the tents are arranged in tight rows. Patrick tells me that not all the sites have such a rigid layout, but this one had significant space constraints. There are two types of tents that people stay in based upon their status at the camp. Established residents receive their own personal tent, each of which is raised off the asphalt on pallets and covered with a tarp. It's obvious that they are well-adapted to the wet climate in Seattle. The tents are labeled by a number on a paper plate that is placed inside of a sealable plastic bag and then pinned to the front of the tent. Prior to receiving one's own tent, newcomers must spend a probation period in a shared, group tent. These larger shelters are created using standard carports with a foundation of plywood on top of wooden pallets. Four beds are in each—constructed from milk crates with sleeping bags and blankets piled on top. Carole notes that this initiation process allows for "the weeding out of those who can't or won't follow the rules of the camp."

In addition to the residential tents, there are a handful of community tents. This includes a donation intake and distribution tent, a large gathering area with several tables and chairs covered by a canopy, and one tent with a couch, television, dozens of movies, and a few computers. I am told that the city pays for electricity, the computers, and Internet access, with the primary purpose being to assist in searching for jobs and writing resumes. At the current site, the church that is hosting the camp is letting residents use their commercial kitchen, but Carole tells me that this is not always the case.

The Itinerant Model

The most notable aspect of the Seattle model is that the camps are itinerant by definition. While the communities are required to continuously relocate to various sites, the stability of Tent City 3 and 4 is still significantly improved when compared to the situation in Ann Arbor. Here, the camps are sanctioned, and the time at which they are required to move is known in advance and at set intervals. This allows residents to better plan their moves in a well-organized and less stressful manner.

But the success of this model can be largely attributed to the benevolence of the faith-based community throughout King County—in particularly the network formed by the Church Council of Greater Seattle. This aspect can make the model somewhat difficult to replicate elsewhere, as proven by the efforts of Camp Take Notice. Caleb is a firm believer in the itinerant model based upon his experience living in these Seattle tent cities. He argues that the continual relocation both relieves the burden on the surrounding community and promotes a more transitional atmosphere for the residents within. Furthermore, he points out that relocation requires the tent city to interact with the surrounding community, building a critical network of support. However, CTN was not able to find churches in Ann Arbor willing to commit to the responsibility of hosting a temporary tent city.

Additionally, while the residents of Tent City 3 and 4 have developed creative solutions to the daunting task of moving a 100 person community every three months, I still found myself with a more stable model in mind—one where residents could move out of tents and into tiny houses. But this would require a longer-term site, and likely a fiercer political battle. It turns out that others in Seattle had similar aspirations, so they broke off from the itinerant camps in pursuit of a more village-like model, which they called Nickelsville.

Nickelsville

The formation of Nicklesville in 2008 marked the establishment of a third self-organized camp within the Seattle area. Named after Mayor Nickels, the camp largely replicated the organizational structure of Tent City 3 and 4, but was founded as an attempt at a more permanent, non-moving solution. However, the informal community ended up traveling even more frequently than its predecessors, moving to more than a dozen sites in less than three years.

But in 2011, the camp returned to its original location where it would remain for the next two years. While the site was still unsanctioned, Mayor McGinn vowed to not seek eviction of the camp, and the experiment was finally able to play out. Unlike Tent City 3 and 4, the site was far removed in an industrial location and the development of more permanent features was pursued.

The community described itself as a self-managed eco-village for up to 1,000 otherwise homeless individuals, couples, families, and their pets. At the time of my visit, a dozen wooden structures had been built, with more than 100 tents scattered throughout the site. Those who participated in the construction got their name put in a hat to determine who received each structure. The camp had community support facilities similar to Tent City 3 and also included gardens and goats.

Too the surprise of many, there was also a handful of children living at Nickelsville. I spoke with a single mother who emphasized the safe environment provided by the community when compared to life on the street. She noted that there were other individuals at the camp that took it upon themselves to make sure her and her daughter were comfortable. While she was actively looking for housing, she told me that her daughter actually preferred the camp to the small apartment they were evicted from—there were always other kids to play with and they had built forts and play areas at the camp.

After more than two years at the site, Nickelsville was evicted in 2013 and has since split into two separate communities.

A veteran "Nickelodeon" helps a newcomer secure dry shelter

Maria with her uncle in front of her mother's tent

Chapter 8

St. Petersburg's Charitable Camp

• • •

**What are the costs of institutionalizing
a self-organized camp?**

This case study is actually located outside of St. Petersburg—in
unincorporated Pinellas County—but the camp's roots can be traced to
an impromptu tent city in the city's downtown where police were filmed
slashing the tents of the camp. The video received national coverage
and now has over a quarter-million views on YouTube—establishing
St. Petersburg as "a national poster child for cruelty against the homeless."[79] The ensuing public concern around the issue led to a sanctioned
tent city, known as Pinellas Hope. The event was groundbreaking since
it was the first sanctioned example that was not along the West Coast.
But my visit to the site, which I describe in this chapter, left me skeptical enough to further investigate the origins of the project. Divergent
accounts from two of the key players involved—former Mayor Rick
Baker and the Reverend Bruce Wright—along with thorough coverage
from the *St. Petersburg Times* (now known as the *Tampa Bay Times*)
make for an interesting story, to say the least. But the story is also a very
informative one. Through an in-depth analysis of the establishment
of Pinellas Hope, we begin to see the physical, social, and economical
consequences of adopting a charitable model and institutionalizing a
self-organized tent city.

Entry to Pinellas Hope with common facility under construction in background

A grid of 250 tents with security shacks that view down the rows

Restroom trailer at Pinellas Hope

The Backstory

The Seamless City tells Rick Baker's story during his two terms in office as mayor of St. Petersburg (2001-2010). A chapter of the book devoted specifically to homelessness begins with Baker relishing time spent with his family during his regular Christmas break. "We get pleasure from long mornings with holiday movies and fires in the fireplace. It is one of the most enjoyable and relaxing times of the year for me... with some exceptions."[80] He then expands on one particularly memorable exception that left him "annoyed" in December 2006:

> The morning's newspaper came with a surprise. There was an article with a picture about a transition homeless center on 16th Street, toward the west side of downtown. Over the course of several weeks, some of the area's homeless had taken to pitching tents in the right of way next to the center. At some point, the 16th Street center's leadership decided to invite the homeless to bring their tents into a partially fenced-in area of their property next to their building. In a very short period of time a makeshift tent city had formed...

> ...The worst thing you can add to our "natural attractor" status is a homeless center with no rules! Thus, the makeshift tent city established by the 16th Street center was exactly the wrong approach to dealing with the homeless. The objective for any homeless effort should be to help people work toward independence. In order to accomplish that objective, it is necessary to have rules of conduct. When you open the doors to anyone who wants to come for a free meal and bed with no rules, you quickly become a magnet for people who want to be taken care of without having any responsibility for their conduct.[81]

Baker proceeded to send a notice of code violation to the landowner. He notes that this type of thing "can take months or years to enforce," but in this situation, "those who ran the center chose a different approach."[82] St. Vincent de Paul ran the "center," but apparently their cooperation earned them no specific reference in his book.

Shortly thereafter, in early January 2007, around 150 people were evicted from the vacant land owned by St. Vincent de Paul. Some received 30 day rent vouchers, floor mats at a shelter, or bus tickets out of town, but others did not qualify for or were not interested in these options. Those leftover carried their tents down the street, back to their original location under a highway overpass. But this act still violated city code, and police force was used to make this unmistakably clear by cutting the bases of these meager homes with knives so that they could not be used again. "The problems weren't the people. It was the tents," said the city's police chief. "To me it didn't make a difference if they were the Boy Scouts of America."[83]

This controversial act led many to demand a more ethical solution to the issue. The Rev. Bruce Wright and other advocates pointed to the successes of the original Tent City as a solution, which it turns out was far more organized than Baker portrays it. "This tent community was already a functioning community and working well on its own," said Wright. "They had created their own rules and organization. And, I believe that the powers that be were threatened by the fact that the community could do for themselves."[84]

Prior to the initial eviction, the members of Tent City had composed a compelling letter to the editor in the *St. Petersburg Times* that detailed the success of their self-governance and the potential for this kind of democratic "tent city model." Many of the benefits to living in a tent community described in previous case studies had also been discovered and defended here. "Most of us came alone to the camp. Now we are a community, just like yours, except we live in tents," they write. "All we ask is that you let us stay, let us work, let us keep our community so that we can earn money, find places to live, and help others in our situation."[85] In addition, the website "St. Pete for Peace" became a venue for Rev. Wright and other advocates to document and publicize this citizen-driven initiative.

> ...grassroots advocates will continue to partner with the homeless to create new and innovative solutions that strike at the root of the injustices that create homelessness, poverty and hunger. They remain hopeful that, given the overwhelming support received from

the community, the Tent City model, and the ideas that this model provoked, will not only not be forgotten, but be propagated by all those who are tired of expensive, ineffective and bureaucracy-laden social programs that exacerbate an already dire situation.[86]

Adding more pressure on the city to act, two members of the original Tent City were murdered on the street by a group of teenagers shortly after being displaced from the camp. While this may have been one of the most severe example, violent hate crimes against the homeless are reported to be a common occurrence in the city.[87] As Baker alludes to in his book, the warm winter climate of central Florida leads to an influx of homeless people from colder regions, and it appears some locals see this as an invasion of their town and react hostilely. A growing awareness of the violence heightened the public demand for a safe place to be for the city's unhoused population.

As the "crisis" escalated, Mayor Baker announced a Community and Business Summit on Homelessness that involved all parties with an interest in the issue: municipalities, social services, property owners, church leaders, advocates, and the unhoused. A key outcome of the event was the temporary reopening of a tent city on the same St. Vincent de Paul property. But this time, the land was leased to the city, and Catholic Charities—the largest private network of social service providers in the country—was contracted to manage the camp and to institute rules of conduct that included no input from the residents. Meanwhile, the homeless community and their advocates worked together to re-establish a self-governing camp of their own with 30 tents hosted on church land, but the effort was short-lived after the city refused to issue a temporary use permit.

By May 2007, both camps were closed, but a separate outcome of the Summit on Homelessness remained in place. A series of ordinances had been passed prohibiting panhandling downtown, storing personal items on public property, and sleeping outside. This, along with previous events, led St. Petersburg to be ranked as the second meanest city toward the homeless in the country (Los Angeles was first).[88]

Church and State

Later that year, Catholic Charities proposed a "more sophisticated tent city" to be located on a 10 acre site owned by the Catholic Diocese, which was more than ten miles out of town in Pinellas County.[89] The unincorporated site was adjacent to a cemetery and far removed from other residential uses. The proposed pilot project was to operate from December 2007 until April 2008, serving as many as 250 people at a time during the annual winter influx. Admission would only be granted through referral by a street outreach team that included a police officer paired with a social worker, and after an initial screening was conducted by Catholic Charities at their St. Petersburg office. Each resident would be assigned a tent and a case manager, and be expected to work toward financial independence. A private security firm would provide 24 hour surveillance along with assistance from the county sheriff department. Residents would be required to carry photo identification while on site, and searched each time they entered the site. Busses and vans would also be leased to shuttle residents into town for interviews, jobs, or service appointments.[90]

Rev. Wright heavily criticized this "bureaucratic" model that included no input from the homeless community on how it would be set up or governed. "There are all kinds of red flags about this proposal," he wrote.[91] Advocates and former residents of the original Tent City had proposed a grassroots model at the Summit on Homelessness earlier that year, but it had been entirely ignored by the city. Instead the proposal by Catholic Charities was rushed through all the necessary approvals so that it could be operational that winter. This was a selling point for Mayor Baker, who very much wanted to avoid another tent city debacle in St. Petersburg.

In his book, Baker speaks casually of his cronyism with Catholic Charities CEO Frank Murphy. "Since the Catholic Church owns a lot of land in the county, we asked him if he had any ideas."[92] Murphy's plan was strategically located in the center of the county, which coincided with Baker's preference for a "secluded location" that was "far removed from downtown" so as to not attract the homeless from other areas. In fact, Baker would become one of the tent city's biggest supporters:

Although Pinellas Hope was supposed to close after four months, Bishop Robert Lynch of the St. Petersburg Diocese consented to my request to keep it open. My appeal was given along with an offer by me to help raise private funds to operate the facility until the new fiscal year for the cities and county. We would then seek ongoing government funding. We succeeded in obtaining both the short-term private funds and the long-term government financial support.[93]

A Tour of Pinellas Hope

Pinellas Hope was the first and only sanctioned tent city that I had the chance to visit on my initial trip during the summer of 2010. At the time, I knew very little of the background information provided above. I was just eager to get a first hand account of how they were able to accomplish such a difficult task, and learn the strengths and weaknesses of their sanctioned model.

However, upon arriving at the end of a dead-end street that appeared to be in the middle of nowhere, I was informed that I was not permitted to enter the site (even though previous e-mail correspondence suggested otherwise). A woman informed me, "I can't just have random people walking around this place, for all I know you could be the devil!" Explaining the nature of my thesis project and showing a student ID did not persuade her. Unlike the other camps I had been to, this person was not a member of the community I was visiting. She was a paid staff member, hired by Catholic Charities to manage the camp. The entire site was fenced and littered with ironic "no trespassing" signs, and not wanting to get a trespass citation myself, I was unsure what to do next. But it had been a long drive and I wasn't about to give up that easily.

Loitering around the entrance I began talking with people going in and out of the site. After a good deal of waiting I was able to connect with a volunteer who persuaded the woman in-charge to allow him to give me a quick tour. I had fifteen minutes. The first thing I noticed upon entering was a large board that listed all of the camp rules, and another board where residents were required to check in and out. Moving through the site we came to the tents—all identical and arranged in a rigid, grid plan for as far as the eye could see. There were security shacks along the edge of the grid where guards could conveniently view down the entire row of tents. A couple dozen ubiquitous, wooden sheds called "casitas" had recently been built. I was told the casitas and other accommodations were used as incentives to reward those actively working toward independence.

It was clear that staff and outside volunteers were in charge rather than the residents, who walked around the place with their heads down. Meals were prepared off-site and donated—similar to a traditional soup kitchen—instead of being cooked and shared within. A variety of services were offered on-site including a main office, bathrooms and showers, a kitchen, a computer lab to be used strictly for job searches and writing resumes, and even a classroom where residents could obtain a GED. Each of these services was hosted inside of a modular trailer unit, and I was told that they had been donated by St. Petersburg College. A large, conventional building was under construction that would eventually consolidate some of these functions, and there were plans to add permanent housing units as well.

Evaluation

After posting about my visit on my blog, I received an e-mail from a former volunteer that identified with my experience. He was also turned away until an extensive application was accepted.

> I showed up for my first day of work, and quickly became disenchanted with Catholic Charities. Faith based rehabilitation is big business in Florida, and Catholic Charities was given a huge grant to operate the tent city. However, the grant money was directly tied to successful results... I found out that the motives were strictly money oriented. They needed responsible people to boost their success rate and qualify for additional funding. Make no mistake, that place is run like a business, and the business model is based on privately run jails... We used to call it "cooking the books," and while it is not illegal, it is highly unethical, especially for a religious organization.[94]

Prior to my visit, I had read a lot of criticism of the project—specifically on the amount of taxpayer money that had been spent—coming from a citizen advocacy campaign called "Stop Tent City." I had initially dismissed it as a radical conservative group, but the facilities at Pinellas Hope did seem quite minimal and the land, food, and a lot of labor were being donated. But as of 2010, the camp's annual budget was $2.5 million. Along with multi-million dollar federal and state grants, Pinellas County has permanently allocated an annual $500,000 in funding. The strategic location in the center of the county has also been a boon. Each of the five cities in the county is also a contributor, with St. Petersburg being the largest, budgeting $100,000. The City of Clearwater has even closed their local shelter and has since contributed to the funding of Pinellas Hope.[95] The project is often promoted by supporters as cost-effective when compared to "similar" services. The key difference with these "similar" services is that they put people in buildings.

An initial evaluation of Pinellas Hope released by the county touted the project as an overwhelming success. During the five month pilot project, 371 participants were served and 51 percent (189 participants) were successfully discharged—suspiciously *just* enough to make the claim that *most* people moved on. The evaluation shows that Catholic Charities conducted the data collection and defined the criteria for a "successful" discharge, which includes other emergency shelter. Of that 51 percent, 27 percent received financial assistance directly from Pinellas Hope to pay for initial rent and utilities. Of those with an income, only 8 percent were making more than $1,000 a month.[96] Most telling, in a survey of the initial 371 residents one year later, only 16 percent reported being in some form of housing.[97] Former mayor Baker prefers to stick with the 51 percent, though.

The Charitable Model

Pinellas Hope is not much more than a traditional homeless shelter—the only differences being that it is outdoors and out of town. It provides a prime example of what to avoid in the process of sanctioning a tent city. St. Petersburg turned its back on the grassroots model unveiled by the initial Tent City, and instead instituted a vertically organized camp where a service provider hands help down to a client. Naturally, the physical manifestation of this model is a placeless environment based on the militaristic roots of the grid plan.

I am not trying to make a case that Baker or Catholic Charities do not care about the homeless. At the least, Pinellas Hope still provides a safe place to be off the streets for a large number of the unhoused, and undoubtedly has helped several transition to better situations. But while the plan may make sense rationally, a core problem with this vertical model is that it is based upon preconceived notions of how to help people without ever listening to the people being served. Additionally, it was pursued in a way that accomplished other interests as well. This would not necessarily be problematic if those other interests did not adversely affect the primary intent.

Baker saw the project as a win-win. It was a solution that meshed with his ideology on how to help the homeless move toward independence, while simultaneously removing them from the downtown streets he was trying to revitalize. After all, the subtitle of his book is *A Conservative Mayor's Approach to Urban Revitalization that Can Work Anywhere*, and the Pinellas Hope model serves as a means to this end, where the homeless have little role to play other than to get out of the way of economic interests.

While critiques of organizational structure, design, and location can be subjective, the short-sighted nature of this approach is not. For Catholic Charities, Pinellas Hope meant big business if they could produce the necessary results. Under this purview, providing the unhoused with very short-term rental assistance is defined as success. These solutions may look good on paper, but do little to influence long-term change and are very costly to the taxpayer. The reality of the situation is that a majority of these folks are returning back to homelessness, creating a renewable client base for social service providers.

Chapter 9

Portland's Rest Area Camp

• • •

**What about those who do not fit
a community environment?**

I arrived in Portland just a few days after the local Occupy camp had been set up, and the space was already taking shape as a bustling community. In early October 2011, the protestors had claimed two square blocks of downtown Portland known as Chapman and Lownsdale Square. It was not long before tents filled nearly every square foot of the urban green space, and a fully functioning tent city began to evolve as protestors settled in. General assembly meetings were held each evening where anyone could form proposals and voice their opinions on how the camp should be run. Food was generously donated to the cause, and a volunteer kitchen distributed food to long lines of the camp's inhabitants. The protest community formed an information center, medical clinic, library, and even an engineering station where some worked to improve the physical infrastructure of the camp.

This all seemed strikingly familiar to the camps organized by the homeless that I had just completed my thesis on only a few months prior. But there was one significant difference here—these camps were being publicly accepted. Like many other cities throughout the country, Portland's Mayor Sam Adams was allowing the tents to stay without setting any time limit for eviction, establishing a precedent

Visual barrier made from recycled doors with Chinatown Gate in background

Entry to Right 2 Dream Too with concept plan to the left

Tents for members at the back of the site with rest area shelter in the background

for acceptable public camping. How could a city allow protesters to break an anti-camping law, often by choice, yet enforce the very same law elsewhere on those who have no choice? The Occupy camps were defended as symbolic speech under the First Amendment, but what about those making unintentional protest, living in a tent as a means of survival?

Then, just four days after the initial formation of the Occupy camp, Right 2 Dream Too—a tent city geared toward those experiencing homeless—opened just a dozen blocks to the north. While this may have seemed like a move to take advantage of the precedent set by Occupy, the idea had been in the works several months beforehand.

An Example of Direct Action

Right 2 Dream Too (R2DToo) decided to occupy a vacant lot just over the Burnside Bridge, on a corner adjacent to the Chinatown Gate. Even if you've visited Portland just once, you are likely to have passed by this prominent intersection—leading to what has been referred to as one of the "stickiest and most highly visible" conflicts in the city.[98] R2DToo came upon this high profile site as a result of the property's controversial past. For decades, two buildings housed an adult bookstore on the site, but in 2007—following a series of code violations and reports of criminal activity—the store was forcibly shut down by the city and the building was demolished. The property owner, Michael Wright, sued a city commissioner for selectively enforcing ordinances on businesses that he didn't like, but to no avail.

For years, the prominent corner lot sat vacant and became notorious for attracting public urination and graffiti. But in the summer of 2011, Wright began renting the gravel lot to a couple of food carts, and he had plans for adding a whole pod of carts—a popular trend throughout the city. However, following a complaint, Wright was told the food carts would have to go because city regulations only allow for food carts on paved parking lots. Wright offered to pave the lot, but that would have violated the city's moratorium on new parking lots. He could remove the wheels from the carts, but then a whole series of building codes would kick in. Again, Wright felt the city was selectively enforcing regulations on him, and pointed to food carts on gravel lots throughout the city. City officials recognized that this was true, but asserted that those other instances have not received formal complaints. Fed up with not being able to use his property, Wright told the *Portland Tribune*, "I'll donate it to Dignity Village for a year... I think the city of Portland deserves it."[99]

Dignity Village—a sanctioned community for the unhoused covered in the next chapter—had been operating for over a decade, and a few of the community's founders had been talking for some time about doing something again. Upon hearing about Wright's statement, Ibrahim Mubarak and a few others decided to see what it would actually take to make it happen. Wright set three stipulations that would take a few months to get in order: they had to come up with a way to secure the area, acquire liability insurance, and help pay property taxes. So on a Friday evening in October, after the city workers were done for the weekend, a group of the unhoused and their advocates started to bring materials onto the site. The Rebuilding Center had donated 80 doors that were mounted in an undulating fashion to secure the perimeter of the site while creating an iconic visual barrier. I spoke with one of the advocates who recounted the opening of the site:

> That weekend we had volunteers who knew what our plan was that showed up to set it up. We opened on World Homeless Day, which we felt could create enough of a drive and inspiration for people to make it all come together. We knew that it was going to be an issue. We hadn't asked for permission from the city or the Old Town community. Half an hour after we opened the city was here to tell us of our potential code violations. So we thanked them for their concerns, listened to what they had to say, and told them to come back when they had actual written violations.[100]

The formation of R2DToo was a long planned and carefully executed performance of direct action. The group did not have permission, but they revealed an existing problem in the city and simultaneously provided a service that constructively addressed that problem. While Occupy Portland wasn't a part of their original plan, it played an important role in detracting attention from the camp, and made it hypocritical to enforce code violations while a tent city set up by protestors was being tolerated just a dozen blocks away. After all, sleeping in a tent out of necessity is as valid a form of protest as any other. Originally intended as a way to stick a thumb in the eye of city officials, Wright has since found value in hosting the camp. He notes, "The property was being used as a dumping ground... and now I have an organized group that is keeping it clean, and actually really doing something good—keeping people out of doorways and out of the rain."[101]

A Rest Area Model

The immediate area surrounding R2DToo is one of those peculiar cultural juxtapositions that occurs in many downtowns—the sidewalks and doorways entertain a lively nightlife scene while also hosting large numbers of the city's unsheltered homeless population. As a result, R2DToo was conceived as a "rest area" to provide refuge to those sleeping in difficult and dangerous situations on the streets. The concept is similar to that of a highway rest area, but instead for people with no place else to go. In their own words—"We exist to awaken social and political groups to the importance of safe and undisturbed sleep. Our purpose is to create a place where unhoused people can rest or sleep without being rousted by police or private security and without being under the constant threat of violence."[102]

This is accomplished through an innovative organizational structure composed of both members and non-members. The community is self-managed by 30 members that can stay on site 24/7, and also includes space for 60 non-member to get rest at the site in 12 hour shifts. This allows the compact, urban site to provide safe sleep for up to 150 people per day. Members have their own personal tent while three tarped canopies are marked with designated spaces for non-members to roll out a sleeping bag—one for men, one for women, and one for couples. People can use the rest area for one night or as long it takes to find a better situation.

In order to become a member, you must be voted-in by a majority of the existing members. This comes with the benefit of having your own personal space on a consistent basis, but also requires additional obligations. Members are responsible for the intake and oversight of the non-members each day and night, and must complete eight hours of front desk duty each week. In addition, a RAC (Rest Area Coordinator) position was established to give further responsibilities—such as enforcing the rest area's rules—to elected members. However, the RAC position has recently been abolished to reduce hierarchal controversy within. Instead, any of the 30 members can now enforce a rule with three witnesses. There are also dedicated organizers, like Ibrahim Mubarak, that hold things together when conflict arises, as well as an overseeing non-profit board of directors.

A key advantage of this model is that it provides a safe place to be for a wider demographic than other examples—specifically those who are not apt for participating in the day-to-day life of living in a community. While self-governance empowers residents to set quality of life standards within, it also limits the population being served to those who are socially appropriate. Mark Hubbell, a former member of R2DToo, told me, "For those not actively looking to join a community, this is the perfect fit. You can go in any time during a twenty four hour period, get your rest, and get back up with your stuff and go."

Many of the other models included in this book have more extensive expectations for residents—such as attending meetings and giving back to the community—and those that cannot follow through with these responsibilities are often evicted. Members of R2DToo are held to similar obligations, but non-members only have to abide by a very basic code of conduct. Utilizing the rest area strictly as a sleeping space rather than a living space reduces opportunity for conflict and accommodates individuals that may be more difficult to get along with.

Hubbell came to stay overnight at R2DToo after a few weeks sleeping under the Burnside Bridge. He recalls, "It was something I saw that was providing such a necessary comfort for folks—that 12 hours of uninterrupted rest." Wanting to get more involved, he began working alongside a member in charge of platform and tent maintenance. "At that time we [members and non-members] were all in tents, so you had to go through everyday and clean out all the tents. If they got water in them you had to wipe them out and put back new sleeping bags—just get them ready for occupancy again." He began working under an existing member that became an informal mentor, and after a few weeks, Hubbell was accepted as a member himself and was put in charge of maintenance.

This brings a second key advantage of the model to light—it provides members with a duty and sense of purpose. In exchange for a place to stay, the members manage the provision of a safe place to sleep for others. Hubbell's experience emphasizes the positive nature of this aspect: "It gave you a place to belong, and gave me a sense of purpose. I've always wanted to help so this was the perfect vehicle for that. It gave me something to do to feel good about around the place that I live." He told me of how Mubarak, the rest areas leading organizer, instilled in them that it's not enough that you're homeless, but that you need to learn about being homeless, and you need to speak about being homelessness to give others a first hand perspective of what your life is like. "What I took out of it was this is bigger than me, I'm nobody, I'm the same as everybody else, and if I do one little good thing that helps somebody else, that was the point of the whole deal."[103]

Finding a New Site

R2DToo has existed on the controversial site at 4th and Burnside for over two years now, and in that time several attempts have been made to try and make this not the case. Wright and R2DToo faced reoccurring fines for violating the state's recreational campground ordinance, accruing a bill of more than $20,000. But by December 2012, facing even steeper penalties, a lawsuit was filed against the city on the grounds that R2DToo was a rest area, not a recreational campground.

Nearly a year later, a settlement was reached and the violations were waived. In addition, a new site was identified for relocating the rest area to a city-owned parking lot—sheltered by an overhead bridge—in the up-and-coming Pearl District. The city's Bureau of Development Services issued a zoning decision that authorized the move without being subject to building permits or design and land use reviews. However, the plan was met with significant resistance from the neighborhood—in particularly the leading developer in the revitalization of the area, who warned the city against putting the rest area near their multi-million dollar projects.[104]

The controversy delayed a final decision, and to detract attention the mayor put a vacant warehouse near the existing site on the table, but it was soon determined that costs for making it a habitable structure would be too high. Finally, to extinguish any possibility of locating the rest area in the previously proposed parking lot, the developer mentioned above reached a million-dollar deal with the city to purchase the lot for around $150,000 while funneling $850,000 to the city to find an alternative site for R2DToo—away from their development.[105] The act affirms that R2DToo is likely here to stay, but where exactly remains in question. The property where they are now has been listed for sale.

Organizers and members of the rest area emphasize how critical the central location of the existing site is to the model's success. Several other services are nearby, and it is therefore highly visible to the population they serve. In fact, many had already used the sidewalks on the block as place to sleep before the rest area existed. R2DToo simply allows this to happen in a safer and more orderly environment.

The rest area has become a positive asset in an area known for attracting more than its fair share of police calls. The members take great pride in adding more eyes on the street, and partnering with the police to maintain a safer environment. Along with monitoring the rest area facilities, members also complete regular perimeter checks around the block. Hubbell points out, "There is a direct correlation between R2DToo being where it is, and the decline in police calls to the area. That was part of our outreach... we were visible."

Right 2 Dream Too | Code of Conduct

1) We are a Weapon Free Zone

2) We are nonviolent and will not tolerate violence

3) We respect the rights and privacy of our fellow members and neighbors

4) Degrading, ethnic, racist, sexist or homophobic remarks are not acceptable

5) We cannot permit open flames

Any of the following are grounds for being escorted out of R2DToo:

◊ <u>Alcohol on the premises:</u> Alcohol policy has the consequences of 1st offense 24 hours out; 2nd 72 hours out; and 3rd you are out for good for overnighter or member.

◊ <u>Illegal drugs on the premises:</u> 1st possession is revoked membership status. Must also look at suspicion of being under the influence for overnighters and members—a 72 hour out and out if overnighter.

◊ <u>Violence or threat of violence on the premises:</u> "Verbal intervention"—1st offense is 24 hours out; 2nd offense is 72 hours out and 3rd is revoked membership status. "Physical contact"—1st offense is 12 in 12 out with your belongings; appeal to membership meeting.

◊ <u>Sexual Harassment:</u> "Sexual remarks" has consequences of 1st offense is a warning; 2nd offense 24 hours out; 3rd is back to 12 in 12 out status with your belongings.

◊ <u>Theft of any member's property or R2DToo's Community Property:</u> Revoked membership; Appeal to membership meeting

◊ <u>Open Flames:</u> 1st offense 24 hours out; 2nd 72 hours out; and 3rd is revoked membership status.

All of the above must be logged with an incident report for each infraction.

PART III | VILLAGES

PART III | VILLAGES

DOME VILLAGE

1993-2006

LOS ANGELES, CA

🏠🏠🏠🏠

Site: *private | central | landowner sold property*
Housing: *geodesic domes designed by student of Buckminster Fuller*
Cost: *$10,000 per unit*

DIGNITY VILLAGE

2001-present

PORTLAND, OR

🏠🏠🏠🏠🏠🏠🏠🏠🏠

Site: *city-owned | zoned as transitional campground | 7 miles from city center*
Housing: *custom tiny houses up to 150 sq. ft. | volunteer & resident-built*
Cost: *largely used & donated materials | $25/person/month*

VILLAGE OF HOPE

2004-present

FRESNO, CA

🏠🏠🏠🏠🏠🏠🏠🏠🏠🏠🏠🏠🏠1

Site: *private (non-profit) | zoned as campground*
Housing: *prefabricated tool sheds with two people sharing each structure*
Cost: *donated structures*

RIVER HAVEN

2005-present

VENTURA, CA

🏠🏠🏠🏠

Site: *city-owned | temporary use permit*
Housing: *"u-dome" structures at 120 sq. ft. for individuals & 200 sq. ft. for couples*
Cost: *$40,000 for 19 "u-domes" from World Shelters ($2,100 per unit)*

OPPORTUNITY VILLAGE

2013-present

EUGENE, OR

🏠🏠🏠🏠🏠🏠

Site: *city-owned | conditional use permit | 3 miles from city center*
Housing: *modular tiny houses at 60-80 sq. ft. | volunteer & resident-built*
Cost: *$100,000 w/ in-kind donations (capital) | $30/person/month*

🏠 = 5 Units

QUIXOTE VILLAGE

2013-present

OLYMPIA, WA

🏠🏠🏠🏠🏠

Site: *county-owned* | *conditional use permit* | *4 miles from city center*

Housing: *144 sq. ft. permanent tiny houses* | *contractor-built*

Cost: *$3 million (capital)* | *$87,500 per unit w/ in-kind donations* | *30% of income*

SECOND WIND COTTAGES

2013-present

ITHACA, NY

🏠🏠🏠🏠🏠

Site: *county-owned* | *7 acres* | *7 miles from city center*

Housing: *320 sq. ft. permanent houses* | *volunteer-built*

Cost: *$12,000 per unit w/ in-kind donations*

OM VILLAGE

2014-present

MADISON, WI

🏠🏠

Site: *private (non-profit)* | *planned unit development* | *converted auto-shop*

Housing: *99 sq. ft. tiny houses on trailers* | *volunteer & resident-built*

Cost: *$5,000 per unit w/ in-kind donations*

COMMUNITY FIRST VILLAGE

planning stages

AUSTIN, TX

🏠🏠🏠🏠🏠🏠🏠🏠🏠🏠🏠
🏠🏠🏠🏠🏠🏠🏠🏠🏠🏠🏠🏠🏠🏠🏠🏠🏠🏠🏠🏠🏠🏠🏠🏠🏠🏠🏠🏠

Site: *private (non-profit)* | *27 acre masterplan* | *planned use development*

Housing: *a variety of tiny houses, RVs, and teepees*

Cost: *$6 million / $30,000 per person (capital)*

EMERALD VILLAGE

planning stages

EUGENE, OR

🏠🏠🏠

Site: *N/A*

Housing: *modular tiny houses at 120-150 sq. ft.* | *volunteer & resident-built*

Cost: *$12,000 per unit (capital)* | *$150-200/person/month*

 = *5 Units*

Chapter 10
Portland's Autonomous Village

• • •

**What are the strengths and weaknesses of
authentic self-governance?**

In September of 2000, Portland's *Street Roots*—a newspaper written and sold by those experiencing homelessness—published the front-page story: "We Need a Tent City." The editorial was written by Jack Tafari, a homeless advocate who was himself homeless. At the time it was estimated that the city had a population of around 4,000 people going unhoused, yet during the coldest months, when emergency shelter was added, there was space for only about 600 people.

That winter, Tafari and seven others erected five tents on public land, dubbing themselves "Camp Dignity." "We were old and young, black, white, and red; Rasta, Muslim, Christian, and Atheist," Tafari recalls. "We were also freezing cold and fed up with the way things were. It was the first year of a new millennium and we wanted to begin a new beginning."[106] Together they formed the Out of the Doorways campaign based on three core values: "to renounce charity models for responding to poverty, to be self-governing, and to demonstrate the 'practical wisdom' behind the creation of a city-sanctioned campground for homeless people."[107]

The fresh abolishment of a 19 year old camping ban was a key factor in propelling the campaign forward. Passed in 1981, Portland

Municipal Code 14A.50.020 restricted camping on public property and public right of ways. The law broadly defined a "campsite" as "any place where any bedding, sleeping bag, or other sleeping matter, or any stove or fire is placed, established, or maintained, whether or not such place incorporates the use of any tent, lean-to, shack, or any other structure, or any vehicle or part thereof."[108] While the ordinance was justified as a means to protect public land, it concurrently erased the space in which anyone without the right to property or formal temporary shelter must live, which based on the estimation above, was more than 3,000 people.

Nomadic Beginnings

But even with the camping ban lifted, Camp Dignity faced significant hardship in the pursuit of a legal tent city, primarily in the form of NIMBY complaints. However, this homeless coalition knew they were in for a fight from the start and they devised a variety of strategic responses. For example, following an eviction from a site, shopping cart parades were staged as the campers moved their stuff to a new location. These spectacles drew both the attention of the media and the concern of the larger community. *Street Roots*, which had published Tafari's original call for a tent city, was another vehicle for raising awareness by articulating a unified vision for the future of those experiencing homelessness in Portland. Heavily attended meetings began to be held in the organization's office. The group began researching the successes and failures of previous tent cities—such as Dome Village in Los Angeles—and formed a site selection team to scour the city for areas to locate a more permanent settlement.

During these early stages, Portland's tent city movement also gained critical support from members of the housed community who provided expertise in various areas—most notably architect Mark Lakeman and community organizer John Hubbird. With this support, a formal proposal was drafted and submitted to the city that outlined Camp Dignity's intent. The plan—"Dignity Village 2001 & Beyond"—explained why a tent city was necessary, how it would be organized, and what it would look like. The goal was to create a "self-help environment" based on the core values established at the outset of the campaign.[109]

A tiny house at Dignity Village after several additions

The village garden shed

A group working on the raised garden beds at the Village Building Convergence

Previous success of the camp was attributed to the "uniquely organic process" in which the tent city evolved, and the proposal emphasized that this dynamic must remain in place in the future. Through collaboration with architects and designers, the group brainstormed a long list of features desired for the village—including ideas for organic gardens, bike racks, art walls, and a community meeting house. It was proposed that residents move out of tents and into self-constructed, human-scale structures made largely from recycled materials.

Without a more permanent location, however, it seemed impractical to invest in such ideas. To address this, a phased development strategy was devised, starting with very basic arrangements. Each subsequent phase would advance the project's physical infrastructure, ownership status, and organizational development.

◊ Phase One | Nomadic Beginnings: Until more permanent land is controlled, short-term arrangements should be sought with public or private landowners for a minimum of three months at a time. Physical composition includes tents, portable toilets, and ephemeral cooking and meeting areas to accommodate 80 people.

◊ Phase Two | Settlement: With a secure location identified, more involved features may begin to be implemented. While a permanent site is ideal, it is reasonable to start with a land lease of around two years. The features put into practice here should be transportable with temporary utility hook-ups.

◊ Phase Three | Development: A permanent site should be acquired so that more permanent features can be developed. Here, more elaborate common areas are constructed while umbrella roofs and enclosing walls are added around pods of tents.

◊ Phase Four | The Village Complete: Many of the advanced features will be completed, and residents will have engaged in the construction of custom micro-housing made from recycled materials. A long-term plan includes acquisition of an additional site in a rural area to accommodate farming and other micro-enterprises.[110]

Settlement and Development

Overall, the proposal was an effective tool for bringing the village concept to fruition. In September 2001, roughly one year after the inception of Camp Dignity, the tent city was granted sanctioned land for up to 60 people. It was then that one-acre of Sunderland Yard—a city-owned leaf composting facility—was designated as Dignity Village.

For two and a half years the village operated under short-term lease agreements, bending regulations while the city explored other options. During this time, Dignity was able to advance from its nomadic beginnings to phase two of the plan—settlement. At this time several supportive relationships were formed with organizations in the surrounding community. In her article "Faces of Dignity," Susan Finely describes one such partnership with Washington State University Vancouver, which focused on improving educational accessibility for the unhoused. Residents learned to create e-mail accounts, research potential grant opportunities, and maintain websites. At the same time, students experienced diverse fieldwork that met specific degree requirements.[111]

But even with significant public support, Dignity faced eviction yet again in 2004 after a public complaint regarding the lack of enforcement around building codes, which obligated the city to act on the situation. At this point, the majority of development still consisted of very ephemeral, makeshift shelters with little regard for formal codes. Under threat of eviction, an obscure Oregon state statute was brought forth at the last minute—ORS 446.265 on transitional housing accommodations—that states:

> A municipality may approve the establishment of a campground inside an urban growth boundary to be used for providing transitional housing accommodations. The accommodations may consist of separate facilities, in the form of yurts, for use as living units by one or more individuals or by families. The person establishing the accommodations may provide access to water, toilet, shower, laundry, cooking, telephone or other services either through separate or shared facilities. The accommodations shall provide parking facilities and walkways[112]

These accommodations are limited to "persons who lack permanent shelter and cannot be placed in other low-income housing" and can be managed by non-profit organizations or private persons. It allows a municipality to limit the duration of stay and restricts the use to no more than two parcels per municipality. A heavy emphasis is placed on yurts, which are defined as "a round, domed tent of canvas or other weather resistant material, having a rigid framework, wooden floor, one or more windows or skylights and that may have plumbing, electrical service or heat." This is because the statute was part of a larger bill that also eased regulations to allow yurts in recreational campgrounds—a boon for Pacific Yurts, an Oregon-based yurt manufacturer. Other types of structures are also permissible for the transitional accommodations, and are subject to similar regulations set for recreational campgrounds.

So in February 2004, the City Council voted to designate an adjacent portion of Sunderland Yard as a "transitional housing campground." As part of the agreement, the city would cover relocation costs for moving Dignity a short distance to a different section of the same parcel with a newly paved surface and a similar level of infrastructure. The act guaranteed a more stable location, allowing for the advancement to phase three of the plan—development. At this point, physical conditions were drastically improved as residents transitioned from mostly tarp-covered shelters to more durable, wooden structures on raised foundations. Then, after nearly six years of short-term agreements with the city, a three year contract was signed in May 2007.

The Village Complete

Dignity Village is a self-governed community. During my handful of visits and tours of the village, this was a core value that was heavily touted and defended by the people living there. A "village council" of up to 25 members is elected through a vote of all members of the village. Through regular meetings, the council makes important planning and organizational decisions related to the operation and maintenance of the village. To ensure that the council's actions reflect the majority of all members, general village meetings are held bi-weekly where the council receives advice on issues. These meetings are open to the public in order to receive input from the surrounding community as well. Within the council, a board of directors is elected to also run the village's non-profit organization.

The village is a membership-based community. When space becomes available, the next person on the waiting list receives "guest status" for thirty days. In order to become a resident, one must attend all meetings during this time and fill out the admittance agreement form. This internal agreement includes basic rules that promote tolerance and participation, and prohibit violence, drugs, alcohol, theft, and persistent disruptive behavior that puts the community at risk. After another thirty days, a resident may become a member of the non-profit if approved by a vote at the general weekly meeting, which then grants them the right to vote on issues and serve on council.

A 2007 survey shows that the majority of residents were male (70%), white (75%), and between the ages of 31 and 50 (minors are not permitted). The village allows couples to live together and also includes pets—arrangements not permitted by the traditional shelter system. From its establishment in 2001 until March 2007, Dignity reported that over 700 people transitioned through the Village, though comprehensive data on where they transitioned to was unavailable. A frequently asked questions form states that different people stay for different amounts of time based on the individual's personal situation. It was estimated that 25 percent stay for only a few days or weeks, 55 percent stay for several months, while 20 percent stay more permanently and become heavily involved with operating and managing the village.[113]

The admittance agreement asks, "What can you contribute or give back to Dignity?" This represents an important dynamic of the village. Not only are members expected to follow a certain set of rules, but they are also required to give back to the community in some way based on their personal skill set. A minimum of ten hours per week is the expected contribution from each member. As a result, various committees devoted to specific tasks have formed. For example, an outreach committee works to make connections with the larger community and provide curious parties like myself with this kind of information. An intake committee deals with interviewing and vetting new residents. And a sanitation committee is responsible for maintaining a clean and orderly environment. Sanitation is also upheld by renting four portable toilets and two dumpsters, which is one of the few operating costs of the village.

Security is provided through self-policing. Each resident is required to complete his or her share of security duty each week. While on duty, the residents maintain order by enforcing the basic rules and patrolling the immediate surrounding area. However, any resident may submit an "incident report" to the council if he or she witnesses another resident breaking a rule. Between 2007 and 2009, emergency 911 calls from Dignity Village were placed at a rate of 0.22 calls per capita, which was lower than the city average of 0.36 per capita.[114]

At first, the village was funded primarily by private donations and grants. However, as time went on, donations dried up as the excitement behind the project faded, and residents now contribute $25 a month to cover the community's operating costs. For those without a source of income, micro-business ventures have been tried as an alternative source for raising money. This has included seasonal events like the summer yard sale, an on-site organic garden, and producing and selling tie-died clothing. At one point, the community owned and operated a food cart—a popular trend throughout Portland. However, by far the most successful micro-business has been chopping and selling firewood, with the success attributed to the simplicity of the operation.

This model has proven to be an economically efficient method for dealing with the issue of homelessness, with an average daily cost of $4.28 per person per day in 2007. This has been compared with other local programs throughout the city—warming centers averaged at $12.59, emergency shelters at $20.92, rental assistance at $24.60, supportive housing at $32.37, and transitional housing at $66.56.[115] This demonstrates that a self-help approach not only provides the unhoused with dignity, but it does so in a way that is very cost-effective.

As planned, with a stable location residents were able to gradually move out of tents and into micro-housing structures built largely from recycled materials. Each resident was responsible for the design and building of his or her own dwelling with assistance from a construction committee. Single-person dwellings range from around 100-120 square feet while dwellings for couples are slightly larger. The individ-

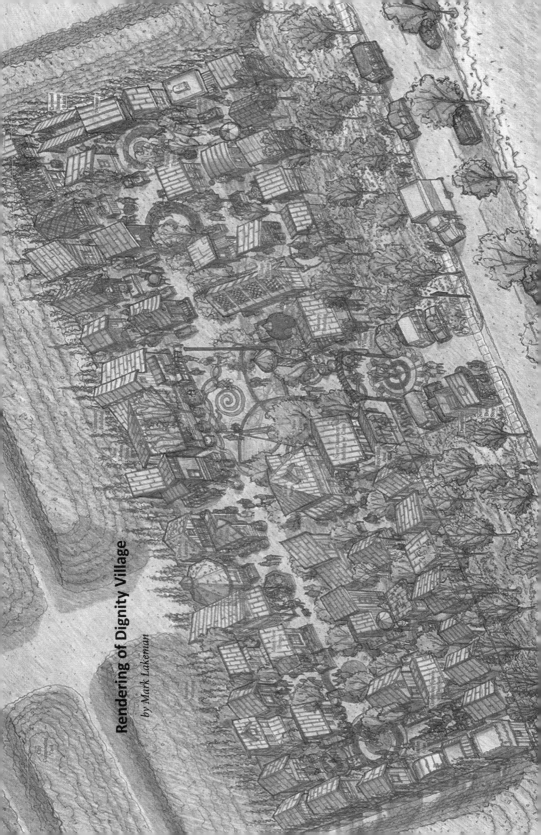

Rendering of Dignity Village

by Mark Lakeman

ual structures do not have water or electric hook-ups. They make use of a propane heating system that was developed by working with the city's fire marshal. An emphasis on front porches was used as a method for promoting social interaction. Other shared elements were also implemented such as cooking facilities, showers, computer access, community meeting spaces, a front office, and a library. A comprehensive village plan was drafted to provide an overall vision for these spaces.

An ecological dimension was also pursued in order to increase self-sufficiency. There is a community garden in raised beds, along with beds in each courtyard space and planter boxes attached to many of the homes. Expanding organic gardening is a goal of the village that can both increase income and provide the community itself with food. Currently residents get most of their food from food stamps, donations, and income from part-time jobs. Cooking and sharing food communally is a regular event, as it is in most tent communities.

Some of the residents have used inverters and batteries to provide personal sources of electricity. Plans for solar and wind based energy have been presented but not yet implemented. Water catchment systems direct runoff from some structures into rain barrels used for gardening. A transition from portable toilets to composting toilets has also been proposed as a more sustainable and economical alternative.

Much of the village planning and design can be attributed to a partnership with Mark Lakeman and the City Repair project, which aims to produce community-oriented places through creatively reclaiming under-utilized public spaces. In 2004 Lakeman received the Lewis Mumford Development Award from Architects, Designers and Planners for Social Responsibility for his work with Dignity Village.

Compromises Made

While Dignity was able to achieve the goal of acquiring sanctioned land, it did not come without compromise. Prior to the move to Sunderland Yard, the camp was located under a highway bridge at NW 18th Avenue and Savier Street. While the physical nature of the camp may have been far from ideal, the central location in the city was. The relocation to sanctioned land displaced the community approximately seven miles from the downtown—a bus commute of around 40 minutes. This is widely agreed to be the primary disadvantage of the community. The initial proposal for Dignity Village identified four specifications that were desired in a sanctioned site:

1) Locate close enough to the urban core so as to be accessible and visible to the homeless population being served

2) Be large enough to accommodate the size and scale noted above (80 residents)

3) Situate near neighbors who are supportive of our goals

4) Provide safe and sanitary environmental conditions (no toxic residues, not too noisy, etc.)[116]

These are fairly basic conditions, but with a quick look at the existing site that was allocated by the city, it is clear that none of these requests were respected:

1) Dignity Village is on the urban edge, far from visible to the population it is serving, which is primarily located downtown.

2) The population capacity was limited to only 60 residents, and many of the urban design strategies for creating a place-based community were not implemented due to the space constraints of the site.

3) Neighbors include a prison, golf course, international airport, and other light industrial uses, which are ill-equipped to be supportive of the community's goals. The nearest convenience store is two miles away, and supportive services for transitioning to traditional housing are located downtown.

4) Being situated directly adjacent to an airport runway results in significant noise and air pollution.

Many members of Camp Dignity were reluctant to relocate such a distance from downtown. Some refused the fenced, one square mile of asphalt, referring to it as a "concentration camp".[117] However, the offer was recognized by the majority of campers as a symbol of the city accepting Dignity as a valid community, and this was something that members of a tent city could not turn down.

Evaluation

Following the three year contract signed with the city in 2007, a third-party evaluation of Dignity was published in 2010 to inform the Portland Housing Bureau on the performance of the village during that time period. It is probably the most empirical data currently out there on this method for responding to homelessness, and overall, confirms its value. The executive summary lists a handful of findings to justify support of the model as well as modifications to strengthen its success. The evaluation lent credence to efforts to renew Dignity Village's contract for another three year term, based on the following findings:

Dignity Village has successfully sheltered 60 homeless people each night, year-round, at a cost per bed night that is one-third the cost of the cheapest shelter option within Portland's homeless services system.

Stakeholders and neighbors affirm that Dignity Village has made substantial improvements in its safety and stability. From 2007-09, the annual rate of 911 calls resulting in the dispatch of Portland Police to Dignity Village was lower on a per capita basis than the citywide average.

During the contract term, the Village replaced all of its tarp and tent structures with semi-permanent structures, significantly improving its livability, its visual impact on the neighborhood, and its code compliance.

The Village has developed and enforced basic rules of conduct, including an improved screening and evictions process that has substantially reduced issues with problem residents.

More than 90% of the stakeholders interviewed for the evaluation supported the City's renewal of Dignity Village's contract. A few of the stakeholders specified conditions under which they would support renewal. These conditions are incorporated into the report's recommended contract modifications.[118]

In an effort to strengthen the village's success and to address the concerns identified by stakeholders, the evaluation recommended a series of modifications. This included better accountability around code enforcement, partnering with other non-profits to provide on-site support and improved organizational development, providing bus tickets to improve accessibility, using a term other than "transitional housing" since the village is distinct from the traditional understanding of this service, and establishing better communication between the city and the village.

Lessons Learned

Dignity Village has existed as an entirely self-managed solution to homelessness for over a decade now, and that alone is an impressive feat. In recent years, however, some have argued that the community has witnessed a period of disinvestment and stagnation. The rate at which residents are transitioning out of the village has slowed dramatically, resulting in a greater number of long-term residents. In November 2012, after a series of short-term extensions, another three year contract was secured. However, this time a two year residency limit was added to the contract (with some exceptions).

The reason for a slower rate of transitioning out can be attributed to a number of factors, the most obvious of which is recent economic conditions. With the recent economic recession, finding a job and maintaining economic stability became more difficult for citizens throughout the country, so one would expect similar trends for those trying to recover from homelessness.

A second factor is the isolated location of the village. While this has been a consistent setback since the beginning, it correlates with a third factor, which is weakened support from the surrounding community. Being on the fringe of the city makes it difficult for existing supporters to get to the village and for potential new supporters to even find out about it. When the village opened, it was such a new and exciting project that many organizations and individuals jumped at the chance to get involved in some way, and it was widely covered by the news media. However, with time, the excitement waned and media coverage became almost non-existent. The village is so isolated that few people would ever stumble upon it unless they were intentionally trying to. And, without relations and partnerships with the outside community, it becomes significantly more difficult for residents within to find a way out.

While it may be difficult for supporters to get to Dignity, the village still has the ability to go to the supporters. This is where the final factor comes into play. Many early residents will tell you that the village has forgotten how to reach out to the community, and that this can be attributed to frequent leadership turnover. In recent years, there has been a significant loss in core members contributing to these kinds of efforts. By core members, I mean residents who truly understand and uphold the founding principles of the village.

In the beginning, the founding members of the community were committed to realizing the vision they had fought so hard for, but with time, they each eventually moved out of the village and on to other things. This was a staggered process, though, so that as some core members left, others still remained to pass on their knowledge to new residents who then wanted to uphold the noble vision. This worked successfully for several years, but some of those who I spoke with pointed to a specific time in the recent past where a large turnover took place. Several core members moved on within a short period of time, resulting in a lack of leadership and a damaging impact on the organization and management of the village.

In setting out to plan a similar project in Eugene, Oregon—known as Opportunity Village—we knew it would be imperative to learn from these weaknesses. Through continued conversations with current and past residents of Dignity Village, we received valuable advice on things that they would do differently if given the chance to start over knowing what they know now. The most frequent and heavily stressed recommendation was to not emulate their membership-based non-profit organization structure.

At Dignity Village, the members of the non-profit are composed of the residents of the village—meaning that the residents elect a board of directors and can amend bylaws. While this structure allows for a purer form of self-governance, it can also be detrimental to an organization when a large turnover in membership occurs within a short amount of time, as just described. And since by definition the members of this kind of organization are supposed to be transitional, a high turnover rate can be expected. This means that the original vision for the village could be discarded if a majority of newer residents prefer different rules—creating a truly organic and autonomous community.

While I am personally intrigued by the mere existence of such a community today, it limits the ability to put an effective and durable model in place for transitioning people out of homelessness. Instead, core members of Dignity advised that we form a board-only non-profit organization with a board of directors that is separate from the village but still includes representation. This allows for organizational decision-making to occur in a more stable environment, and better ensures the continuation of the original vision as long as board members are selected diligently.

A second common piece of advice was to have smaller dwellings. We were informed that larger personal living spaces encouraged residents to isolate themselves, and lessened the likelihood for social interaction and growth. This was seen to be damaging to the community as a whole. Consequently, they recommended we use even smaller dwelling units and focus more on creating useable community spaces where the village could gather.

One of many cats at Dignity Village

Chapter 11

Olympia's Formal Village

• • •

**How does government funding influence the
grassroots nature of a self-organized camp?**

A group known as the Olympia Poor People's Union first
established "Camp Quixote" in a downtown parking lot in February
2007. The city had recently passed a new ordinance that prohibited
sitting, lying, panhandling, performing, and selling things within six
feet of a downtown building. The camp's name draws a fitting reference
to Don Quixote—the infamous literary hero who gleefully sets off on
delusional adventures in the name of chivalry—for Camp Quixote
was about to embark on a six year journey in pursuit of more civilized
treatment of the city's unsheltered population, with many adventures
along the way. Despite being portrayed as a naïve fool, Quixote is widely
admired as a dreamer that has come to symbolize the pursuit of high
ideals without distraction of material concerns or the limits of reality.
And so "Quixote Village" became an imaginative vision in the distance.

But first, lets start from the beginning. As all of the previous
examples have demonstrated, it takes persistent direct action to warrant
formal recognition, and the case in Olympia was much the same. The
pages that follow include an abbreviated narrative of the first days of
this journey written by Ray Kavick, an early member of the camp.

Tiny Houses at Quixote Village

Common facility with tiny houses to the right

Dining and living room in the common facility

The first tents were awkwardly set up with the people at the campsite looking over their shoulders every once in a while. I felt that many of us were waiting for the police to come immediately. During the planning meetings, it was assumed by nearly everybody that we would be at the site for an hour at most. When the first five tents went up and an hour had passed, none of us were completely sure what to do. But that soon passed, the group got together and we decided to go ahead and put as many tents and as many people on the site as quickly as possible...

...By nightfall, the group was operating smoothly and the unity we had talked about and hoped for in the meetings was materializing. Once the fear of the police had subsided, we all threw ourselves headlong into the undertaking and the sense of excitement among the group gave us all a small, constant buzz. We were no longer doing something "illegal," we were doing what we needed to do. If something needed to be taken care of, people got up and did it. Whenever someone needed something, we gave it to them, or tried to. At the end of that day, the hope I had for the encampment multiplied exponentially.

The next day, in our local newspaper, we were on the cover. The Olympian was telling everyone that we set up the camp to "protest" the new laws. While all of us despised the laws, we did not do this to "protest" anything. We did this to create what we needed: housing and a sense of community. But it was easier for the Olympian to label us as "protesters," something they are still doing.

Anyway, that day brought the media, along with more people, more food and more tents. There was no word on the police, but in the paper the City Council expressed anger at us for being "ungrateful" for all the City had done for the "homeless"... We set up a communal tent to store food and serve as a makeshift kitchen. An Olympian photographer and reporter wandered through the camp. The City manager, Steve Hall, came by and informed us that this action represented a "poke in the eye" to the City...

...It was ridiculously cold that second night. A few people brought a barbeque down and some coals, being that burning a fire to keep warm was forbidden to us. Later, even burning coal was made "illegal." The cops had started driving by regularly earlier that day, going up and down the alley next to the camp. It got down to 22 degrees Fahrenheit that night.

The next three days brought us a number of things which I will tackle in no meaningful order. A communal hall was built with lumber donated from a local salvage company; it was draped in tarps and became an awesome little spot for us to hang out. Our kitchen was expanded and a fantastic fellow acted as our cook... In the hall we had communal food and tobacco, with new donations coming all the time. We shared everything there. A few people were a little reluctant to share their tents and some people got mad at the positioning of certain tents, but the problems were handled without much friction. I have not felt so at ease in a long time. I will probably say it again, but this was a small slice of the kind of community and future many of us dream of. Some of you may give me shit, but I wanted to cry a few times for absolutely no rational reason...

...On the second-to-last day the police gave us written warnings to leave or face arrest. On the back of the warning was a list of numbers for shelters that the residents of the camp could call. All of them were either out of service, full or impossible to get into quickly. After that, we began to look for another spot to house the encampment. A church was contacted and it seemed likely that they would let us. When the word finally came that we could in fact move to the church's property we informed the City that we would be moving. Nevertheless, the State had to flex its muscles and surround the encampment at 4:30 Friday morning. We were basically out of there already and we finished cleaning out the spot under the eyes of the cops. We left the spot cleaner than we found it.

Now we're at a new spot in West Olympia, being graciously put up by the Unitarian Universalist Church. They are not dogmatic and are truly good people. While the camp is no longer Downtown where more people can get to it, we still have a safe place to go. The community and the bonds that grew out of that first week are still alive and strong.[119]

To avert the dispersal or arrest of refugee campers, the Olympia Unitarian Universalist Congregation invited the group to set up camp in the parking lot of their church. Following this, Olympia eventually adopted a "temporary homeless encampment" ordinance that allowed a camp to reside on land hosted by a religious institution for up to 90 days—similar to the precedent already set in Seattle—on grounds that both the federal and state constitutions protect the free exercise of religion. From there, seven different congregations hosted Camp Quixote on a rotating basis for the next few years.

The camp maintained a population of around 30 residents, and like its predecessors in Seattle, remained dedicated to self-governance and direct democracy despite being hosted by religious institutions. A "resident council" was responsible for admitting new residents and removing residents who could not abide by the camp's rules. With the local success of the model, the city and county have since approved a maximum stay of 180 days at a single site.

From Camp to Village

Sancho Panza was Don Quixote's loyal companion who voiced practicality along the way, and thus Camp Quixote's non-profit partner took the name Panza. The organization grew out of the dedicated volunteers from the various faith communities, and became a faithful side-kick to Camp Quixote focused on public relations, volunteer coordination, and fundraising.

In 2012, Panza had a $56,000 budget for operating the 30 person camp. The largest cost was a part-time "resident advocate" contracted from Catholic Community Services, responsible for connecting camp residents with available resources ($20,154). All other expenses went toward camp operations with the largest annual costs being sanitation ($7,913), insurance ($7,201), maintenance/upgrading ($4,393), moving expenses ($2,934), and propane ($2,251).[120] The bulk of funding was supplied by Thurston County with supporting private donations. Camp residents were also expected to contribute $15 a month to cover basic supplies, collected by a resident elected as treasurer.

Along with moving the camp every 90 days, Olympia's ordinance went further than Seattle's by also requiring 24 hour volunteer staffing of a "host desk." According to Jill Severn, a Panza board member, this burden turned out to be an asset in that volunteers developed close relationships with camp residents, providing personal growth opportunities for both the housed and the unhoused. "This is where our political power came from," Severn told me.

But as time wore on, volunteer and donor fatigue set in. From the beginning the rotating camp was viewed as a temporary solution, with a long-term vision for developing a more permanent site. For the first few years, measures to ensure the mere survival of the camp required full attention, but by 2010 Panza found capacity to refocus on the initial goal and presented a plan for transcending from Camp Quixote to Quixote Village.

More than three years and $3 million later, this vision was ultimately realized—albeit more expensive than initially anticipated—when camp residents got to move into a village of tiny houses in late December 2013. Let's take a look at the planning and process for getting there, particularly with regard to the influence of significant public funding on the grassroots tent city model.

Planning the Village

Like Dignity Village, the management plan for the village was based on a tradition of direct democracy that had matured over Quixote's years of experience as a self-governed camp. Through a learning process of trial and error, a clear division of responsibility and authority developed between the board of directors, resident council, and an elected executive committee. Panza emphasized the importance of respecting the autonomy of the residents in governing and managing themselves, and only intervened in camp affairs on two conditions: if the camp requested assistance or if rules were not being followed.

This original organizational structure was carried over from the camp to the plan for the village, but with a some significant alterations. Most notably, Panza and Quixote undertook a more formal landlord-tennant relationship and additional staff was hired. Along with the half-time resident advocate—responsible for helping residents set goals and connect with resources—the village also includes a full-time program manager—responsible for oversight and administration of village operations—and a maintenance and janitorial position. So in the transition from camp to village, the community became more of a hybrid model, where paid staff are responsible for the operation and maintenance of the site in partnership with a commitment to self-governance and resident autonomy.

As for the design program, Quixote Village follows the village model by combining small private spaces with shared community facilities. Severn noted that it was important to camp residents to retain the balance of privacy and community founded in the original tent city, and so rather than subdivide a large building into isolated units, the program included 30 tiny cottages (140 sq. ft.) facing a common open space. While completing volunteer shifts at the camp, an architect worked with residents to develop the design for the village. A distinctive feature of the program is that all of the support facilities—including a kitchen, dining room, living room, meeting space, staff offices, and restrooms with showers—are conjoined in a single building (4,000 sq. ft.). This resembles a more traditional take on a congregate living facility. The program also included a workshop building (800 sq. ft.), a covered picnic area (350sf), and 11 parking stalls.

Public Process

Following the initial planning stage, a lengthy public process ensued with many obstacles to surpass. How could this quixotic project meet the formal demands of reality? To help answer this question, Panza contracted with an experienced affordable housing developer, Community Frameworks, to act as the project manager and fiscal agent.

It was June 2010 when Olympia's city council first tasked the land use and environmental committee with finding "a permanent site for the homeless." From there, the committee recommended that the council direct the planning commission to expedite amendments to the zoning code in order to allow for the development of "a permanent homeless encampment as envisioned by Panza and Thurston County" on two acres of county-owned land. The undeveloped land was located in a light industrial area with no adjacent residential uses, and was formally selected for the following reasons: county ownership and support, buildability, and proximity to a bus line, jobs, and a community college. Furthermore, the use was supported as consistent with the city's comprehensive plan and the site passed an environmental assessment.[121]

The city council agreed to the recommendation and the planning commission recommended allowing the unconventional land use—30 small dwellings supported by a community gathering facility. This was accomplished by making it a "conditional use" under the allowable residential uses in a "light industrial district." So it was an amendment to the city's zoning regulations rather than a site specific rezoning—meaning this type of development could technically occur as a conditional use on any county-owned land that is zoned industrial and is not adjacent to residential areas. The decision was appealed as non-compliant with the state's Growth Management Act, but was ultimately upheld and incorporated into the city's comprehensive plan.[122]

Olympia Municipal Code 18.50 was amended to expand the ordinance that already allowed for "temporary homeless encampments" to also include stipulations for a "county homeless encampment." While the former ordinance only allowed for temporary encampments on land hosted by religious institutions, the latter allowed for a permanent site on county-owned land. Along with requiring a conditional use permit, the ordinance includes a number of other stipulations and requires that all structures meet standard building code.

By April 2012, the hearings official approved the conditional use permit for Quixote Village, though a series of appeals dragged the process out further. The project was opposed by surrounding business owners and the Industrial Zone Preservation Association, who felt the location would adversely affect the industrial district as well as the village residents. It was appealed primarily on grounds of incompatibility and traffic impact. First, it was argued that the area exceeded regulatory noise limits, however it was found that this regulation was intended to protect two abutting zones, not different users within the same zone. It was further noted that the site was not any louder than pre-existing encampments, and that resident testimonies found noise to be the least of their worries. But to address the concern, a condition was added to notify incoming residents prior to move-in that it was a high-noise area. The other complaint was based on adverse traffic impact and called for adding a connecting paved sidewalk, restriping the road, and a minimum of 22 parking spaces.[123] These appeals exemplify how petty arguments based around obscure regulations are often pulled in to indirectly support other unspoken concerns that are less politically acceptable—a common occurrence in projects including homeless and low-income people. Additional conditions were added, though less stringent than the complaints called for, and the conditional use was ultimately upheld.

Panza leased the two acre site from Thurston County for 40 years at one dollar per year. While the project is distinct in allowing a permanent development from the beginning, the "encampment" is still not formally recognized as a permanent housing alternative for the residents. The conditional use decision states: "Though permanent structures and facilities are proposed, Quixote Village will remain a temporary home for its residents. The goal of Panza is to transition residents from the encampment back into the community. Social service is provided to this end."[124]

Government Funding

The initial vision for Quixote Village outlined a local community funded initiative. The idea was for individuals, organizations, or faith based communities to be able to sponsor one of the 30 tiny houses. Their plan states, "We anticipate that the cost per cottage will be about $5,000—an amount that would be within the capacity of local groups or individuals." It also called for the central community building to be funded by foundation and business association grants, and to form partnerships with local organizations in an effort to develop a village garden and income generating projects.[125] This early funding strategy lays out a means to develop an alternative form of housing independent of public funding. However, in the pursuit of building the village, this grassroots strategy was radically abandoned.

The project first received $1.5 million from the state's housing trust fund—a funding source devoted to the construction of affordable housing—to pilot a "demonstration" for a low-cost housing alternative. Following this, Panza brought in Community Frameworks as a fiscal agent. From there, the experienced housing developer was able to secure Community Development Block Grant funding from both the county and city. So, in reality, the funding for the development turned out to be 88 percent government funded, with just 12 percent coming from private cash and in-kind donations.[126] The grants acquired for the project required the development of permanent infrastructure, which is why a 40 year lease was necessary. Furthermore, they required that development meet minimum quality standards—often seen as a roadblock to tiny houses. But the development was able to meet the standards set by a local single-room occupancy (SRO) code.

In all, the capital budget for the project stacked up to just over $3 million, or around $105,000 per unit. When accounting for the donated land from the county and some professional in-kind donations, the real cost came to $2.6 million, or $87,500 per unit. Operating and service costs were estimated at $7,000 per unit—a monthly cost of $585 per household.[127]

The High Cost of the Formal Route

A primary consequence of substantial public funding was that the project had to strictly follow a formal development process, similar to that of conventional low-income housing construction. This resulted in a divergence from the volunteer and resident-built model executed by Dignity and Opportunity Village. Instead, professionals were contracted to construct the village over the course of six months, and residents moved in once the development was finalized. Some residents contributed to the design of the village, but professional specialization does not consider the occupant—or the volunteer—to be a practical participant in the home building process. Labor costs were further driven up because the development required prevailing commercial wage rates, which are significantly higher than residential rates. Stormwater drainage standards required significant site excavation and grading that also contributed to the development costs.

Furthermore, the process resulted in a standardized built environment with 30 identical tiny houses, aside from being painted different colors. The use of a single design greatly simplifies construction and permitting costs, which were already remarkably high considering the scale of development. So not only does formal development result in excessive costs, but it does so in a way that severely limits individuality and inextricably diverges from the organic process on which the self-organized tent city is founded.

At $87,500 per unit, the project has been touted as inexpensive in comparison to the average cost of new low-income housing construction, which is often estimated at upwards of $200,000 per unit. But because of how small scale of a project this was, the proportionally high costs expose the inflated nature of the building industry. This is often difficult to grasp in the context of large and complex buildings, but the absurdity of the status quo becomes transparent in the formal development of a 140 square foot tiny house. Quixote Village is therefore a testament of how the formal development process has become an inherent impediment to truly affordable housing.

This is not to say that there were no advantages that resulted from the funding. The physical conditions and accommodations that were implemented far exceed any other example in this book. Each unit is wired with electricity and has a plumbed bathroom, and the common building is comfortably finished to conventional standards. This is certainly an achievement for a humble tent city!

But we must not fall into the same trap of contemporary affordable housing, where development is tied to standards that diminish accessibility due to dependence on subsidy. After all, the limited amount of funding allocated is a reason why affordable housing is in short supply in the first place. A principal advantage of the village model is that a local community can carry out an alternative form of affordable housing in the absence of governmental capacity—and that aspect must be preserved for advocate groups without access to this kind of funding.

That said, I believe Quixote Village offers an exemplary model for working within the current confines of public funding stipulations. Panza did far better in preserving a significant degree of resident autonomy in comparison to Catholic Charities' management of Pinellas Hope. However, the next case study attempts to find a better balance between the formal development process and the constructive informalities of the self-organized camp by implementing a grassroots strategy similar to the initial plan for Quixote Village.

Tiny houses all in a row at Quixote Village

Kitchen in the common facility

Chapter 12

Eugene's Collaborative Village

• • •

How can a community meet formal expectations
while preserving positive informalities?

By now, the Occupy movement has been all but forgotten by most. But in Eugene, Oregon, the protest sparked an inadvertent undertaking in the form of a self-managed, transitional housing community, known as Opportunity Village. The earliest roots of the village can be traced to the local Occupy camp formed in August of 2011. Like many cities, Eugene witnessed the emergence of a robust encampment with democratic assemblies, volunteer-run clinics, and makeshift kitchens serving hundreds of meals each day. But, also like many other cities, the informal settlement soon took on an unplanned dynamic—specifically, a safe and secure place to be for the city's unsheltered population. Suddenly there were more than 100 otherwise homeless individuals, couples, and families living and interacting with a group of otherwise housed activists. The camp was relocated throughout the city on several occasions, but as time passed, more people came to take refuge in this new community—that is, until late December of 2011, when the camp was shut down shortly after a violent fight erupted on the site. Suddenly it seemed that the great experiment in a more democratic society was laid to rest once again.

The first volunteer building event at Opportunity Village

30 foot wide yurt heated with pellet stove

Tiny houses under construction

But all was not lost. The events had succeeded in catalyzing public concern around confronting the issue of homelessness. The unhoused and housed had gotten to know each other, and the seeds that had been planted during the various democratic assemblies soon found light.

Growing a Village

Following the closure of the Occupy encampment, Eugene's Mayor Kitty Piercy appointed a task force to identify "new and innovative solutions" for approaching homelessness. Known as the Opportunity Eugene Community Task Force on Homeless Solutions, the group incorporated a diverse range of citizens that included representatives from neighborhood associations, the local school district, non-profit agencies, the police department, and local business owners, as well as housed and unhoused representatives from the camp. After a series of meetings, the group put forth a list of recommendations in April 2012, with the number one recommendation being: "Direct city staff to work with community members to identify potential sites in order to establish a safe and secure place to be, opened by October 1, 2012, independently financed with oversight by a not-for-profit organization or agency."[128]

It was then that the seeds for a village began to germinate. While the task force did not come to consensus on a specific vision for this "place to be," an advocate group—composed primarily of those inspired by what took place at the Occupy camp—continued to meet informally to ensure that this recommendation was in fact implemented. Known as the Homeless Solutions Committee, the group began to further develop a vision for this place to be, establishing the foundational root network for a self-governed, transitional housing village.

At this point I became regularly involved with the project. I had just moved to Eugene for a job a few months prior, and the coincidence of my arrival coinciding with energy growing around the very topic on which I had just completed my thesis appeared to be fate. As I became involved in these conversations, lessons learned from the local Occupy camps began to merge with much of the research on self-organized camps presented in my thesis project. The long-standing, sanctioned examples in Portland and Seattle became case studies from which to learn and grow, and St. Petersburg exemplified what we were trying to steer clear of. Early conversations focused around self-management, alternative micro-housing, relations with the surrounding community, and transcending from the negative connotations of a "camp" to the positive optimism of a "village"—an "Opportunity Village." The strategies for getting this issue on the table are further discussed in Chapter 14, Advocating for a Village.

The Concept

The Occupy camp largely operated under an ethos of unregulated autonomy, and therefore lacked any widely accepted rules or boundaries. This allowed people with malicious intent to prey on the community, inflating a negative impression of the camp in the surrounding community. In contrast, while Opportunity Village aimed to encourage individual autonomy in many ways, it also recognized the importance of enforced community agreements—as demonstrated by other self-organized camps—in order to maintain a certain quality of life internally and to establish trust externally. And while the Occupy camp accepted anyone and everyone, it was decided early on that members of Opportunity Village must be vetted and able to abide by a basic set of rules.

While the sanctioned communities in Seattle and Portland had 60 to 100 members, it was decided that Opportunity Village should have a smaller population of around 30 to 45. We felt that this would encourage a more direct means of decision-making while still maintaining the capacity to run a self-managed community. However, to more adequately address the scale of homelessness in our area, we decided that there should be a network of these small-scale villages.

Our initial proposal included four villages of 30 people each, but after receiving public input we scaled the effort back to a 30 unit pilot project. The plan called for micro-housing supported by a shared kitchen, gathering space, front office, and restrooms with showers. Oversight would be provided by a non-profit organization, and similar to existing examples, self-management would be employed to uphold basic rules prohibiting violence, stealing, and alcohol and drug use on site, while also encouraging tolerance and participation. It would be emphasized as transitional housing with a goal of moving residents to more permanent living situations and serving a larger population, but because everyone's situation is unique, there would be no set limit to the duration of stay. Further details on the planning and design of Opportunity Village can be found in Chapter 15.

The Site

During a January 2013 city council meeting—after months of advocacy and planning—a motion was passed to "Authorize the city manager to take the steps necessary to locate a pilot project for a low-cost micro-housing project for homeless individuals at the city-owned North Garfield site for a period not to exceed October 1, 2014." The steps to be taken by the city included: 1) selection of a non-profit to operate the pilot project, 2) enter into a lease agreement with that organization, and 3) consult with that organization as it prepares an application for a conditional use permit for the site. Furthermore, the lease was to include terms that required: 1) insurance to protect the city against liability, 2) the site to be fully restored by end of lease, 3) a nominal fee for leasing the site.[129] By this point, our advocacy group had evolved into a 501(c)3 non-profit organization, known as Opportunity Village Eugene (OVE), which was selected to operate the project.

Similar to other sanctioned examples, the approved site was in an industrial area; however, the location was less isolated than others. Located within the Trainsong neighborhood, the site is one block from a bus stop and walking or biking distance to a wide variety of services. The site was once a trailer park that had since been repurposed for city vehicle storage. The two acre parcel was subdivided with the front acre designated for Opportunity Village and the back acre remaining utilized for vehicle storage with a fence erected to separate the two.

There were existing plans to develop a city storage facility on the site, but at the time, there was no funding to proceed with the project. Consequently, the land was approved to host a temporary pilot project, which—after going through the necessary steps for acquiring a conditional use permit—would amount to just over one year. The conditional use permit was approved with no opposition present at the official hearing, and the project has since received unanimous support from neighbors and city officials. Nine months after opening, Lt. Eric Klinko of the Eugene Police Department stated, "It has gone better than I thought it would. [The village] has not been a burden to the neighborhood in terms of a crime impact."[130] Furthermore, Claire Syrett, the city councilor who represents the ward in which the village exists, endorsed the project:

> From everything that I have seen and heard regarding Opportunity Village Eugene, it seems to be a great success, in terms of their goals and the commitments they made to the residents of the village, the neighborhood and the City Council... I have received zero complaints regarding Opportunity Village.[131]

A Formally Informal Village

Opportunity Village aims to strike a balance between the informal—as embodied by Dignity Village—and the formal—as embodied by Quixote Village. For example, we borrowed significantly from Dignity Village's venerable system of self-management and governance. Their low-cost operation was developed over a long period of time, largely by the residents themselves with the materials available and under the radar of formal regulations. It is a testament to what homeless individuals can do for themselves, and should be truly respected for that. However, due to both the location of the site and the structure of the organization, the community is isolated and inaccessible.

On the other hand, Quixote Village has found a way to implement a similar concept through the formal development process. While the village has a similar origin as Dignity in a self-organized tent city, it received significant government funding and was built by a contractor with little involvement of the residents—with a capital cost of $3 million. However, unlike Pinellas Hope, a strong emphasis on self-governance was maintained even with the addition of outside paid staff members. This can be attributed to the strong bonds developed between residents and advocates during the years as a democratic tent city. While some aspects of the initial vision were compromised, Quixote Village offers a streamlined approach for implementing a similar model with less dependence on the participation of the residents or the surrounding community.

In my opinion, Opportunity Village falls somewhere between these two examples. A primary goal of the community is to bridge the existing gap between the housed and the unhoused. The village is self-managed and governed in a manner similar to Dignity, but with a close relationship to a separate non-profit organization that includes board members and volunteers from the surrounding community.

Rather than an on-site caseworker, the village attempts to build social capital by connecting residents with relationships and mentors in the local community. This is based on the philosophy that meeting ten people can be more effective than simply turning in ten applications, especially in a tough economy. To this end, the villagers have developed a "Watch Opportunity Work" program—a feature on the OVE website that connects members of the local community with villagers based on their skills, needs, and goals. This has allowed villagers to find occasional work to help pay the $30 monthly utility fee that sustains the community. Furthermore, local teachers and professors have recently started an education program at the village—offering courses on a variety of subjects to villagers and other unhoused people.

By harnessing the skills and resources available within the local community, we were able to divert the formal development process. Instead, residents, volunteers, and skilled builders worked together to develop the village incrementally over the course of nine months on a shoestring budget. After receiving a key to the site in mid-August 2013, we held a "big build" event in which volunteers and residents erected five tiny houses, built ten raised garden beds, and dug a 200 foot trench at two feet deep to run a water line to where the kitchen would eventually stand. Following the construction, around a dozen of the first residents moved in. This core group had already been meeting bi-weekly in the months leading up to the opening. From there, new residents were brought in incrementally, and often moved on site in tents while their shelters were being built. It took a couple weeks to run electricity to the site, and months to complete all of the common facilities.

But by May 2014, the village was built—including micro-housing, a gathering yurt, common kitchen, front office, tool shed, and bathhouse with flush toilets, a shower, and laundry room. I choose not to call it complete since it is a living environment where existing and future residents will continue to make modifications and additions based on need and desire.

The city did not simply turn a blind eye to the project, but instead worked with our non-profit to develop creative solutions for making this informal concept fit within formal regulations. They were incentivized to provide flexibility to accommodate the project since it addressed a paramount issue at no cost to the city other than the provision of land. The plan and structures were required to meet code and undergo permitting, but a number of unconventional practices allowed for low-cost development—including not being required to have a licensed contractor, not having plans stamped by a registered architect, not having to meet excessive requirements for permanent foundations and insulation, and being allowed to build the village incrementally with volunteer labor. In essence, returning the home building process to the people, similar to a good old-fashioned barn raising.

The initial temporary nature of the site created a unique design challenge—to build a village of structures that could be relocated if necessary, while making them substantial and attractive enough that no one would want to move them. Due to the limited duration of the pilot project, electrical and plumbing infrastructure was limited to the common facilities rather than each individual unit, similar to Dignity Village. Consolidating utility hook-ups helped to significantly reduce permitting complexities and expenses. Chapter 16, Building a Village, offers detailed information on the structures at the village along with more on the building process.

As a result of this informally formal approach, the village has been able to be funded entirely by cash and in-kind donations from private individuals, businesses, and organizations. Following the completion of the village, we had received donations of $500 or more from 38 individuals and 20 businesses and organizations. The housing structures cost between $1,000 and $2,000 each to construct, allowing for some donors to sponsor an individual unit.

In addition, the grassroots approach elicited thousands of hours and dollars of volunteer labor and donated materials. Subtracting in-kind donations, the entire village was able to be built for around $100,000—not far off from the per unit cost at Quixote Village. Granted, the facilities at Opportunity Village are less formal and with fewer amenities, but with the $3 million required to develop Quixote Village, this route could house approximately 1,000 people at a time.

What's Next?

In the first nine months of operation, 57 people called Opportunity Village home for varying lengths of time. During this period, 24 people departed from the village with 14 leaving voluntarily and 10 being expelled for rule violations. Several others have found part-time work since living at the village but are still unable to afford an apartment. This means they must either find a better job or receive government subsidized housing—both of which are in short supply.

So, with one complete, OVE is now planning and fundraising for a new kind of village. While Opportunity Village focuses on transitional housing in an effort to serve a larger population, Emerald Village will provide more attainable and sustainable places to transition to. The idea here is to build long-term, affordable housing based on a similar grassroots model. By continuing to build small and utilize local resources, the village can divert the limitations of conventional affordable housing.

An initial concept plan calls for 15 tiny houses at 120-150 square feet each with electrical hook-ups, heat, and a kitchenette. Similar to Opportunity Village, the housing will be supported by common gathering, kitchen, and restroom facilities. Residents will tentatively make $150-200 monthly payments toward utilities and a share of the village. This concept of an "Affordable Village" is further described in the next chapter.

PART IV | GUIDE

PART IV | GUIDE

Chapter 13

A Tent City Urbanism

• • •

There is no one size fits all solution—people are diverse and so must be our shelter. A tent city urbanism takes a bottom-up approach to the provision of shelter, informed by the positive dynamics found in tent cities organized by those experiencing homelessness. This contrasts the currently narrow definition of "home" defined by middle-class values, which has effectively cut out the most affordable sector of the housing market. Consequently, the various case studies covered thus far have been synthesized to define an ecology of community-based housing alternatives that may appeal to various sectors of the population—including the chronically homeless, the recently homeless, the very low-income, and even those who are not constrained by income.

In an effort to guide the aspirations of camps seeking sanctioned status, the actions of advocates and supporters, and the initiatives of cities looking for alternative solutions to shelter and housing, I have set forth a spectrum of models built from the best practices compiled in this book. The models include the Sanctuary Camp, the Rest Area, the Transitional Village, and the Affordable Village. Together, these models provide a more comprehensive understanding of home with a common respect for autonomy and privacy within a community. It also recognizes that different folks have different needs and desires. Some just need a place to catch their footing, others may be at a point in their lives where they do not have the mental or physical capacity to be financially independent, and still others may be looking to simplify their lifestyle, to pay a more sustainable percentage of their income toward rent, to downsize their environmental footprint, or to discover a more meaningful sense of community. The remainder of this chapter will expand on the dynamics and demand for each of these models.

The Sanctuary Camp

There has been growing support—both from governments and advocates—for a "Housing First" paradigm. The idea here is that the most effective way to confront homelessness is to first put people into permanent housing, with an option for supportive services coming second. Many cities are coalescing on this as the long-term solution. However, at the same time, many local municipalities are saying that the funding and infrastructure is simply not there, and that it is a solution beyond the control of the city. But in the meantime, there are things we can be doing locally now to begin with a "Shelter First" paradigm.

I get that the tent is not seen as an acceptable or permanent form of shelter, and I am not an advocate of the tent. But we can't dismiss it in the absence of other alternatives. This is not an either-or argument, but an acknowledgement that we cannot simply pursue long-term solutions without regard to present realities. Jean Stacey, a friend and advocate here in Eugene, has made a fitting, allegorical portrayal of this imperative with reference to a local, unsanctioned camp known as Whoville:

> The U.S. economy is a major shipwreck and many have fallen or been kicked off the boat. Some of the folks in Whoville were among those who found themselves drowning, found some unused resources, and built themselves a lifeboat. Having been out there drowning themselves, they were well aware there were other folks out there struggling, so they started scooping up some of the other swimmers who were least likely to survive on their own and gave them a safe seat in the lifeboat… We believe if government would stop trying to push the refugees out of the lifeboats… the refugees

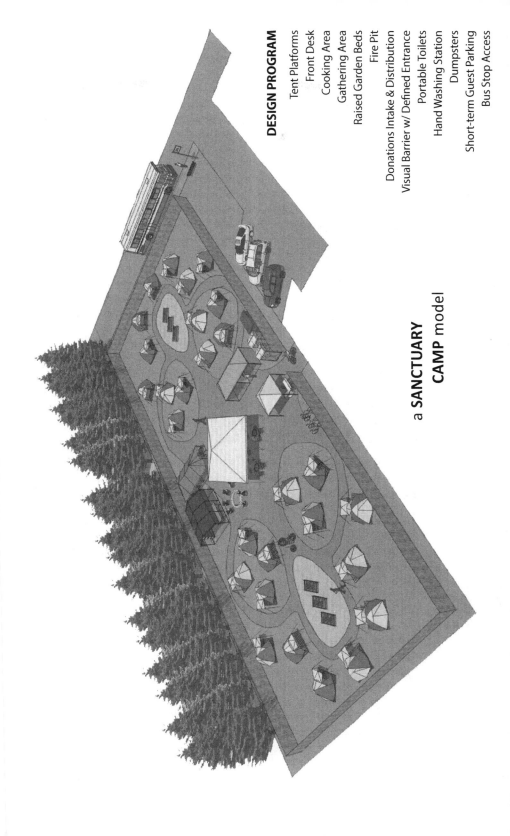

DESIGN PROGRAM

Tent Platforms
Front Desk
Cooking Area
Gathering Area
Raised Garden Beds
Fire Pit
Donations Intake & Distribution
Visual Barrier w/ Defined Entrance
Portable Toilets
Hand Washing Station
Dumpsters
Short-term Guest Parking
Bus Stop Access

a **SANCTUARY**
CAMP model

and the community could float the lifeboats. The government could then form private/public partnerships for the sturdier, longer lasting ships to be built for the long haul.[132]

There is extensive research showing that poverty related concerns—such as the question of where one will sleep on a given night—consumes significant mental resources and limits the capacity to focus on other tasks. Furthermore, quality of life crimes—such as sleeping in doorways or urinating in alleyways—can easily lead to a debilitating criminal record. Together, this reality can make homelessness a self-perpetuating condition that is difficult to recover from. Simply providing a stable place to be from the beginning can make all the difference. It is often the first step in positively addressing the issue—not only humanely but also economically by reducing demands on city services. The Sanctuary Camp model fills this niche.

Ann Arbor's Camp Take Notice, Seattle's Tent City 3 and 4, and Portland's Right 2 Dream Too all provide excellent yet varied approaches to the Sanctuary Camp model. The common thread is that they each provide a safe place to be to the city's unsheltered population while respecting the common desire for autonomy and privacy. Each is self-governed—with emphasis on a regular weekly meeting—and each has formed community agreements that residents must abide by in order to maintain residency at the camp. This commonly prohibits violence, theft, and drug and alcohol use on site, and requires residents to contribute back to the camp through hosting the front desk, site maintenance, cooking, gardening, or any number of other supportive activities. Such camps offer low-cost, citizen-driven alternatives in the absence of federal, state, and local resources to adequately address the crisis of some not having a legal place to exist.

The Sanctuary Camp has a considerably ephemeral built environment that accommodates flexibility in location and duration. In addition, the model can be further defined to accommodate specific demographics—such as a "wet camp" for those still struggling with addiction. However, the experiences at Eugene's Whoville camp present a strong case for a mixed-population with the capacity to form an internal support network.

Tent cities already exist in most every urban area, yet all but a few are currently illegal and subject to eviction. Their mere existence demonstrates our failure to formally meet the basic needs of all citizens, and that this inevitably leads to people coming together to informally develop their own solutions. Rather than continuing to criminalize the collective efforts of the homeless, municipalities should work with the members of tent cities and their advocates to develop viable, temporary solutions that respect the residents' autonomy while meeting formal concerns of the city—at least until longer-term solutions can be carried out. The allocation of sanctioned land allows the unsheltered to further stabilize their lives, reducing the high costs of criminalization, incarceration, hospitalization, and sleeping in doorways and alleys.

The Rest Area

A Rest Area provides safe sleeping space to a more transient population. While the other models presented here are based around self-governance and community agreements, the Rest Area provides a place for those who may not be considered socially appropriate for living in community. By designating an area as a part-time sleeping space rather than a full-time living space, it reduces the potential for conflict and accommodates those who are more difficult to get along with.

This concept was pioneered by Portland's Right 2 Dream Too, and has since been piloted in Eugene under a local "rest stop" ordinance. Portland's example combines the Rest Area with a Sanctuary Camp that includes full-time residents as well, while the example in Eugene is solely a Rest Area. I have found combining the concept with a Sanctuary Camp to be more successful since the full-time residents can help manage and mentor those staying on-site for shorter periods of time. Here, full-time members stay in individual tents, while the non-members sleep in large, group tents marked with individual sleeping spaces that include sleeping bags. While conditions are far from ideal, the idea is to make things as simple as possible to get the most people off the street with a limited amount of resources.

I have separated the Rest Area from the Sanctuary Camp here because it is a component that I think can be added to the Transitional and Affordable Village models as well. In addition to getting more people off the streets, a Rest Area can provide village residents with responsibility and an accompanying sense of purpose. This expands the scope of the other models from simply providing people with a place to be, to creating an opportunity for them to give back by serving those in a less fortunate position—an aspect that is proudly emphasized by members of Right 2 Dream Too. In a village model, Rest Area conditions could be improved from large group tents to an enclosed structure with a series of individual sleeping spaces—similar to what was once known as a "flophouse."

The Transitional Village

The village model provides each person with a small, private space within a community supported by shared, common spaces. It emphasizes local control and broad participation. But what exactly is meant by a *transitional* village? Transition is defined as the passage from one form, state, style or place to another. Therefore, the Transitional Village is not a final resting place, but rather a stepping-stone on which to stabilize one's life before moving on to something else. But what exactly is that something else?

Traditionally, transitional housing is offered for a defined period of time, and is seen as a means to an end—getting the client to sign a lease for permanent housing. The housing type typically involves several rooms within a larger residence, and clients are required to participate in formal support services that assist with addiction rehabilitation, psychological assistance, and job training. Funding is based upon success, which is measured by the ability to place the client in permanent housing.

The Transitional Village model has a similar goal, but takes a less hyper-rational approach in getting there. It provides a more do-it-yourself alternative by providing individuals with responsibility and ownership over a space of one's own within a supportive community of people in a similar situation. Like the Sanctuary Camp, it is founded on an ethos of self-management and governance, with basic rules that residents must abide by to maintain residency. However, the village

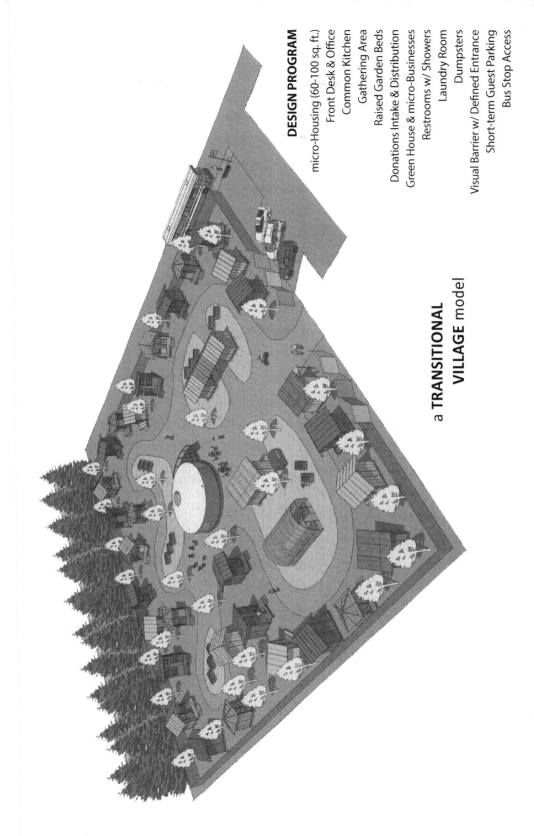

DESIGN PROGRAM

micro-Housing (60-100 sq. ft.)
Front Desk & Office
Common Kitchen
Gathering Area
Raised Garden Beds
Donations Intake & Distribution
Green House & micro-Businesses
Restrooms w/ Showers
Laundry Room
Dumpsters
Visual Barrier w/ Defined Entrance
Short-term Guest Parking
Bus Stop Access

a **TRANSITIONAL VILLAGE** model

provides improved infrastructure by allowing for the progression from tents to micro-housing units that are supported by more substantial common facilities. This model is exemplified by Portland's Dignity Village, Eugene's Opportunity Village, and Olympia's Quixote Village with varying degrees of autonomy, formality, permanence, and cost.

Similar to dormitories or assisted living centers, this form of development can be classified as a "congregate living facility" since the housing is supported by shared facilities. Here, the micro-housing should be designated as "sleeping units"— a space that can provide provisions for sleeping, living, eating, and either cooking or sanitation but not both—rather than "dwelling units"—which have more stringent requirements for being independent. Sharing functions can reduce permitting requirements, costs, and environmental impact.

As demonstrated by both Dignity and Quixote Village, a Sanctuary Camp can evolve into the Transitional Village model, either on the same site or at a different one. Both models can also work in tandem with one another to serve different populations. While the Transitional Village contains a more developed built environment, designing structures so that they can be disassembled or transported intact can make this model suitable to short-term sites as well—as exemplified by Opportunity Village. This establishes flexibility and a more fluid style of urbanism. For example, say there is public support for affordable housing on a vacant parcel of land. A transitional village could act as a placeholder for that development during the lengthy process before construction begins, and later relocate to a new site. Building the structures on trailers is another alternative suitable to temporary sites.

Considering the unconventional nature of this form of development, most cities will likely want to start with a pilot project—one that can be easily abandoned if it fails or extended if successful. This is an understandable precaution, and can benefit both the internal community and the surrounding community. A temporary site eases the concerns of neighbors, and allows time for public input that should be taken into account when evaluating if the project and site will be renewed. In addition, the questionable future of the community can encourage solidarity within, incentivizing residents to come together to make the project a success. Also, if the community is beginning to stagnate, a move could reinvigorate the village, raise awareness and support, and provide a fresh start. But if morale is positive and public support is present, the village should remain stable and enter into a longer-term lease agreement so that it can take on more permanent features. In this scenario, structures could be designed with the ability of being moved on a trailer, and then dismounted on a raised or permanent foundation depending on the site.

While formal services are not necessarily offered on site or required by this model, partnerships can be developed with complimentary service providers in the larger community and made available to the residents. Since part of the intent is to be able to fund a housing alternative within the local community, it does not have to compete with other services for already thinly stretched state and federal dollars. The Transitional Village does, however, require that each resident participate and contribute to the community in which they live. So, rather than help being handed down by a caseworker, the model emphasizes tolerance, peer support, horizontal organization, and participatory culture to re-engage the individual socially. In addition, it can provide a place for building social capital by encouraging relationships between the housed and the unhoused through various efforts.

It is important to note that this is not necessarily an argument for one form of transitional housing over another, but a recognition that a broad range of responses are necessary to address a multifaceted issue. To this end, it is critical to recognize that this also holds true for permanent housing. The Transitional Village is therefore not only intended to transition people to more permanent living situations, but also to act as a vehicle for transitioning to a more sustainable vision of what those situations may look like—long-term affordable housing based upon a similar village concept! After all, if the Transitional Village is fully realized, members of the community will already be living an exemplary lifestyle in terms of social and environmental sustainability. And in a moment when reducing carbon emissions has become widely accepted as indispensable in the wake of climate change, why are we encouraging a move from the village to conventional apartments and houses that are less sustainable on a number of fronts?

The Affordable Village

The reality of the situation is that the rate of homelessness is out-pacing the ability to develop conventional affordable housing. In fact, the demolition of existing affordable housing is outpacing the construction of new affordable housing in most cities—to the point that we are taking one step forward for every two steps back. This is largely due to the creation of a system where new development hinges on government subsidy, while funding for public housing has witnessed decades of decline.

In addition to a growing homeless population, many *with* housing are paying an unsustainably high percentage of their income for that right. More than half of all renters are now paying more than 30 percent—the standard for being considered "affordable"—meaning a large number of working citizens are living paycheck-to-paycheck, one unpredicted expense away from losing their housing. Further still, there is a growing demographic of people looking to simplify their lives, reduce their ecological impact, and strengthen social bonds with neighbors. All of this points to the need for alternative housing options beyond the single-family house and apartment complex.

The Affordable Village meets this demand through the re-establishment of a low-cost and low-impact housing option. It appeals to those without a home, those who could live a more stable life devoting less of their income to rent, those with a desire to consume and pollute less, and those wishing to avert the social isolation of conventional housing by living in a community rather than a commodity. It aligns with the trend in "Housing First" programs, but by continuing to build small, share resources, and utilize economically creative practices, it provides a model that is substantially less depended on public funding.

This differs from the Transitional Village in that it is intended to create long-term housing. The Affordable Village moves to larger housing designs with capacity for more individual accommodations. The units are still supported by shared facilities, but with a lesser degree of dependence. For example, the housing could be electrically wired to include a heat source and kitchenette while still being supported by common gathering and cooking areas. Plumbing each unit is an option, but this can be a big expense depending on the existing infrastructure

DESIGN PROGRAM

micro-Housing (120-160 sq. ft.)
Common Kitchen
Gathering Area
Raised Garden Beds
Restrooms w/ Showers
Laundry Room
Dumpsters
Resident Parking
Bus Stop Access

an **AFFORDABLE VILLAGE** model

on the site. Madison's OM Village provides an alternative that utilizes a composting toilet in the unit supported by a common restroom facility with flush toilets and showers.

Furthermore, the Affordable Village has a smaller population that is intended to offer a higher quality of life—though some may still find a larger population to be more desirable. This is possible because there is less need for internal management in this model, which does not require residents to host a front desk or adjudicate rules. Regular meetings are still necessary, but are focused more on how to maintain and share the common facilities, with a social organization more closely resembling a cohousing community. But the Affordable Village provides an alternative to the popular but costly cohousing and condominium developments, which opens the door to a variety of affordable co-operative ownership structures.

The Transitional Village is still an important asset and compliment to the Affordable Village in that it can serve more people by emphasizing a transitory mission. Whereas the Affordable Village is designed to have a more stable population, the Transitional Village has greater capacity to serve those without access to housing. In addition, it could provide a useful vetting process for selecting residents that will be a good fit for the Affordable Village model. The Affordable Village offers both a step-up from the Transitional Village, or a step-down from housing that may be economically, socially, or environmentally unsustainable. This creates a compelling mix, reminiscent of the camaraderie and collaboration discovered at the Occupy protest camps—once again blurring the line between the housed and the unhoused.

Eco-villages, cohousing, and high-end tiny house communities offer the next stage in this ecology of alternative housing options. The first two have been well-explored by already housed populations wishing to live more sustainably. Cohousing has been successful because it largely adapts to existing regulations, and eco-villages because they prefer rural environments with less regulations. Tiny house villages—for all income levels within the urban setting—are the next frontier.

Chapter 14

Advocating for a Village

• • •

For an advocacy group on the path to establishing a safe "place to be" for the unhoused, the first step is to ensure the issue is part of the public conversation. Homelessness is already a highly vocalized issue in many city council meetings and public forums. If presented well, the village model can offer a fresh take on these often worn out conversations by providing a tangible, low-cost solution rather than an ideological debate. This chapter covers strategies for getting the issue on the table in a way that minimizes public skepticism, scrutiny, and NIMBYism with specific reference to my experience with Opportunity Village.

Developing a Vision

In beginning a campaign, it is essential to articulate a clear vision with achievable goals in order to communicate the project to decision makers and the larger community. Doing so can also clarify direction and establish unity within the advocacy group. What is it that you are trying to achieve? What are the intentions of the village and how are they different from existing services being provided in your area? One method for writing a vision is to have each member of the group write his or her own statement. Then as a group, identify the common themes among the various responses, and consolidate those themes into a concise vision statement.

It is important to keep the statement direct and to the point so that it is something people will read and remember. Rather than trying to fit everything into the vision statement, try to limit it to the main points the group is trying to convey. Those main points can then be expanded upon in an accompanying list of goals that one can read if intrigued by the vision. Referencing and learning from existing models that are successfully accomplishing a similar vision can also be useful. A vision statement for Opportunity Village Eugene (OVE) has been included on the next page followed by our goals that describe how the vision is to be achieved.

Defining a vision and goals will allow your group to establish an identity by sending a consistent message to the larger community. Furthermore, it can protect your sanity by ensuring that everyone participating in the group is on the same page. To this end, identifying the core values of the group early in the process can also be beneficial. To implement the village model, often you will need to make some compromises in order to develop a project that works for all parties involved. Core values establish dynamics that you are not willing to negotiate. They are the cornerstones of the village you want to build. The core values should emerge from the previously set goals and progress to provide measurable objectives.

Once these items have been developed, decision-making becomes easier. Ideas that align with the group's vision, goals, and core values are to be pursued, and those that don't are not. This can reduce backtracking for new members and stonewalling by existing members, while still enabling a collaborative effort. If the conversation is drifting from the point, you can question how it relates to the vision, or if an inappropriate policy is being proposed, you can point out how it contradicts a core value of the project. The composition of these items also provides an effective way for communicating your initiative to others. Process models like Non-violent Communication and Principled Negotiation can also be useful tools at this stage, but are beyond the scope of this guide.

Opportunity Village Eugene | Vision Statement

Opportunity Village Eugene is a collaboration between the housed and the unhoused providing stable and safe places to be through cost-effective, human-scale approaches for transitioning the unhoused to more sustainable living situations.

◊ Collaboration between the housed and the unhoused: By joining together as peers, we form citizen-driven initiatives to create positive changes in attitudes, policies, and practices that harm the unhoused. In doing so, we provide opportunities for volunteers to positively impact the quality of life for everyone in our community.

◊ Stable and safe places to be: By working in partnership with local municipalities and the surrounding community, we secure stable places to be for the unhoused and low-income. Safety is maintained through community agreements that all residents must abide by along with oversight provided by our non-profit board of directors.

◊ Cost-effective, human-scale approaches: We hold a strong belief in self-governance and management in an effort to engage members of our community while minimizing operating costs. A dedication to building small and sharing resources allows for low-cost, low-impact development while still providing each with a space of one's own.

◊ Transitioning the unhoused to more sustainable living situations: Through a combination of peer support, skill building, opportunities for income generation, and connections with community resources, we provide a variety of means for transitioning to more permanent living situations. During changing economic times, we also strive to transition to a more sustainable vision of what those situations may look like.

Get others on board

Once you have a good idea of what your group wants to achieve, meet with local policy makers and community leaders that can make it happen. Without broad support your idea will likely remain just that. Finding the right people to endorse your project can make all the difference. Here, it is useful to have members of the group with strong political connections and the dedication to schedule and follow through on meetings with those connections.

During the summer of 2012, we organized more than 50 meetings here in Eugene specifically on the intent of OVE. This included meetings with the mayor, city council members, city staff, leaders in the business and faith communities, and a number of other influential figures around town. The goal of these early meetings was to establish allies in the community that could strengthen the political credibility of our advocacy group.

Our initial pitch received overwhelming support, but not without its fair share of criticism. Sometimes we were able to clarify misconceptions held by critics while other times they offered helpful advice for how to make the project more attractive to a wider audience. In response we adjusted the scale, location, and language of the proposal, while remaining committed to our core values. Nearly everyone liked the idea of a "hand up" rather than a "hand out" model, but it was heavily emphasized that it would have to look good in order to be accepted by neighbors. To this end, people were enamored by the "tiny house" approach. By combining the goal of providing homes to the homeless while also pursuing a cute form of alternative housing with substantial curb appeal, we seemed to have a marketable proposition.

However, gaining committed support through an initial meeting is not always easy, especially for an unconventional project such as this. At the least, it introduces others to your vision and puts your project on the political radar. After all, it is hard to make progress if policy-makers are unaware of your intent. In the remainder of this chapter, I provide a number of tactics for better positioning your project and heightening the demand for action.

Speak their language

Many groups have bold visions for what a more socially just city should look like. However, it is imperative to not stop after only answering the "what" question, but to continue forward by investigating the "how" question. If you only tell your city that a safe place to be for the homeless is needed, you are unlikely to get the desired results. Governments often must facilitate solutions, but they rarely lead them. It is imperative for the advocacy group to take the initiative to lead government to the solution by telling them *how* to implement the type of project you are proposing.

When asked how the vision for Portland's Dignity Village could be realized, Mark Lakeman emphasizes the importance of speaking the language of those you are trying to relate to. One method is to adopt existing goals and policies of the city or region. For instance, Dignity Village was positioned as a project that would meet new sustainability measures and goals that had recently been locally adopted. And so in our initial proposal of Opportunity Village, we conveyed how our project aligned with each of the "seven pillars" defined in the city's "Envision Eugene" plan. By aligning your project with larger, existing goals it becomes more difficult to dismiss.

In working with Eugene's city officials and staff to implement Opportunity Village, I found that the majority of them were supportive of the concept, yet skeptical that it could be formally realized. Having the know-how to draft proposals that meet formal demands can make an idealistic concept seem more pragmatic to this audience.

Know the Code

In order to make a persuasive case, it is important to be familiar with building codes and zoning regulations for your area. Sure, the idea may sound nice, but how can it be done legally? The village model that I have laid out is founded on the informal organization of illegal camps, so making the argument for how it can be formally accepted is a tough one. Fortunately, here in Oregon, we were aware of a state statute—ORS 446.265—that permits up to two transitional housing campgrounds per municipality, which provided a basis for our building officials to interpret the project we were proposing.

While this statute helped provide formal direction for how to proceed with the project, there are other ways that progress can be made as well. In Seattle, sanctioned tent cities have been defended on church land under the Religious Land Use and Institutionalized Persons Act (RLUIPA). Olympia passed a zoning amendment to incorporate Quixote Village. OM Build in Madison, Wisconsin builds tiny houses for the unhoused, and by putting the structures on trailers and keeping them under 3,000 pounds, they are able to avoid formal regulation. In terms of putting multiple tiny houses on a site, they have pursued a planned unit development (PUD). Ann Arbor's Camp Take Notice is also pursuing this route for the piece of property that has been purchased. A PUD often involves a cumbersome public process, but nonetheless reserves opportunity for unique plans such as these.

These projects are in a grey area, that is for sure. But it does not mean that it cannot be done. It simply means we need to be more creative in pursuing a solution. Codes and regulations are written to prescribe a defined solution to an identified problem but they include a degree of ambiguity when applied to various situations. By understanding the intent of the code there are a range of ways to interpret it when adapting the code to a specific project. It is important to recognize that the planning and building department will likely not do this work for you, and it is up to your advocacy group to determine what interpretations are needed for your project.

The principal concerns of the code are life safety provisions and structural integrity. This intent should not be compromised, but if you are finding that the code is hindering your project for other reasons, you should have a valid argument. By combining the emergency of homelessness with citizen-driven solutions at little cost to the city, you should be in a position to get a more generous interpretation or even an exception—you just have to make it in the city's interest to do so. This was not necessarily the case in the past, but as the issue of homelessness persists and grows as government budgets continue to tighten, more cities are becoming open to alternative solutions that require flexibility in existing regulations.

Identify potential sites

Proposing a specific site is a very effective—though often controversial—way to get the issue on the table. After the advocacy group defines some basic site criteria, survey the city for potential sites that meet that criteria. Most cities have interactive zoning maps online that can assist with this search. By proposing a site, it makes the project relevant to a greater number of people, which is therefore likely to result in local media coverage. The stories are often geared toward initial reactions of the surrounding neighbors to the site, and while they may not be positive, at the least the concept becomes part of the public conversation. Meeting with neighbors and explaining the vision of the project prior to announcing anything publicly can also help mitigate the situation. While some may be opposed no matter what, including neighbors in the conversation early on can go a long way to ease surprise and build respect.

Opportunity Village | Site Criteria

◊ Access to public transportation (within ¼ mile)

◊ Access to public utilities (water, electric, wastewater)

◊ Borders that can be controlled

◊ At least one acre in size (for 30 unit development)

For Opportunity Village, we initially proposed a central site within a residential area. The vacant, three acre parcel was juxtaposed between a church that was supportive of the project and an elementary school with parents that were not so supportive, to say the least. Our meetings with various politicians and community leaders culminated in a meeting at the school adjacent to the proposed site. Here, we were met by ferocious parents determined to keep their children safe from the menacing, homeless boogey-man. They feared for their children's safety and well-being, arguing that their children should not be exposed to "a bunch of people either drunk or high on drugs" or subjected to "the smells of a homeless camp." While it was certainly a difficult event to witness, the controversy landed us in local headlines, and it was then that Opportunity Village became a noteworthy story to cover. We truly felt that we had more support than opposition in the neighborhood, but as is common, those in opposition were far louder. We ended up backing away from that specific site and refocusing on the concept of our project. While some folks were opposed to the site, we found broad support for the concept. In fact, some of the parents who were our biggest opponents stated publicly that there was a definite need for this kind of service, just not next to them.

Finding politically acceptable land is one of the most difficult tasks of establishing this kind of land use. It is common for any kind of new development to be met by NIMBY opposition, and in this case, it is amplified by preconceptions and stereotypes about the homeless. The important thing here is to not become attached to any one site, but to maintain a basic list of site criteria that a site must meet. I never actually felt we had a good chance of getting the initial site we proposed, but like any good bargain, I knew it was a good idea to start high. The event established general public support for the project, though it was yet to be determined where they would support it being established. Finding an answer to this is no easy task, but if enough pressure is put on the city it increases the incentive to find a suitable site.

Utilize complimentary direct action

Historically, direct action has been required for social change to be taken seriously by politicians and the public, and this holds true here. An unsanctioned camp that stays together despite a persistent eviction process calls attention to the fact that existing policies are proscriptive rather the prescriptive. When the issue is simply relocated instead of addressed—especially in a publicly visible manner—it generates increased pressure for determining a legal and ethical resolution.

It is well known that naming something builds emotional attachment. The most common example is the notion that giving an animal a name can make it more difficult to slaughter for eating. Similarly, a camp identified by a name can become more difficult to evict without an alternative solution. The simple act of establishing an identity can further escalate the political controversy and the demand for action that is just. The camp is no longer a group of unrelated homeless individuals, but a community of people in exile. In fact, all of the sanctioned examples in this book have direct roots in a preceding community that was unsanctioned but politically organized.

The establishment of Opportunity Village was less direct than others. While the initial demand originated with the Occupy tent city, the initiative was largely driven by housed activists in the year following the closure of the camp. Despite a formal task force recommendation and advocate-based efforts, the political process for establishing a "place to be" was still moving slowly. City staff had been directed to identify public sites for the project, and came back to council with a list of over 400 potential sites. Jean Stacey, an original board member of OVE, saw this as a stall tactic and decided it was time for more direct action.

Up until this point, the plan had been formally pushed—primarily by housed activists—in what Jean described as the "country club approach." We recognized this as an obvious shortfall of our campaign since all sanctioned examples in other cities included persistent, direct action before demands were met. However, many unhoused friends from the Occupy camp had since found housing through relationships developed with housed protestors—the type of social capital we felt warranted a project like Opportunity Village.

As a result, Safe Legal Entitled Emergency Places to Sleep (SLEEPS) was formed when Jean decided to break off from the group to help organize a critical mass of the unhoused community. This new organization, separate from OVE, was meant to be what Jean described as "the baseball bat behind this search in the desert." SLEEPS took an even more bottom-up approach for demanding a safe and legal place to be for all citizens, and didn't wait for the city to give them the green light. Clusters of tents popped up in visible locations throughout the city, sending a simple and direct message: it is illegal for many citizens to sleep. This escalated the public conversation around what to do about the city's homeless situation, and with no extra government funding to put toward the issue, OVE was left holding the answer. Shortly thereafter, the city narrowed the extensive list to five possible sites—the direct action had greased the wheels of the formal process.

Build a prototype shelter

Seeing is believing! If you are having trouble gaining traction, moving the physical project along as much as you can independently can be an effective strategy. To this end, going ahead and building a prototype of the shelter you are proposing can gather momentum. Start by determining a design for a micro-housing unit that your advocacy group wishes to pursue. Most municipalities already allow for the construction of auxiliary structures without permit, provided that they are under a certain square footage (for example, in Oregon the limit is 200 square feet for a residential property and in California it is 100 square feet). Putting it on a trailer also diverts the building code and allows you to promote your micro-housing around town. While it may not necessarily be legal to inhabit the structure at this point, progressing from a plan to a real life structure can be a monumental step in making it happen.

Prior to establishing a legal site, OVE funded the construction of the "Conestoga hut." This 60 square foot structure was simple and economical, aiming to do the most with the least amount of materials. To raise attention, the hut was trucked around town on a trailer to various events, including an appearance in the park blocks just outside of a city council meeting. This coincided with an impromptu tent city erected by representatives of SLEEPS at the adjacent Free Speech Plaza. The juxtaposition was difficult to ignore—a visible problem placed directly next to a prominent solution going unused—right as the council was about to meet to discuss the homeless problem for the hundredth time.

During the meeting, a motion was passed that approved a specific site to be designated for a pilot project. Concurrently, the council moved to expedite the inclusion of the Conestoga hut as an acceptable means of shelter within the city's existing car camping program, which allows up to three RVs or tents (and now Conestoga huts) on land hosted by faith communities, businesses, non-profit organizations, and municipalities (since then it has also been expanded to six). This allowed us to incrementally begin to realize the vision for Opportunity Village while the pilot project went through the necessary public process. One of our board members and his church's congregation allowed us to construct three huts in their parking lot as part of the above mentioned program.

A SLEEPS direct action camp that became known as Whoville

Building one of the first Conestoga huts in a church parking lot

Building the first bungalow as a prototype for the village

The folks that came to stay there became involved in the planning of the village, allowing us to gain experience with the concept we were proposing and establish a social foundation before the village opened.

The huts really captured the heart of Eugene, and we quickly began to raise money and bring in volunteers eager to contribute time, skills, and materials. Within the first couple weeks of constructing the prototype, we raised over $20,000 to build more micro-housing, and were flooded by phone calls and e-mails from people wanting to help in some way. Following this, we began to also construct a variety of compact "bungalows" made from prefabricated wood-framed panels. These structures would provide more substantial shelter options at the village. OVE started renting warehouse space to store donated materials, and a few prototype bungalows were constructed around the city as demonstration structures that would later be relocated to the village once the site could be legally opened. More details on both the Conestoga huts and bungalows are provided in Chapter 18, Building a Village.

Form a non-profit organization

It is important to continue to develop your advocacy group along the way with the ultimate goal of registering as a 501(c)3 non-profit organization, or alternatively partnering with an existing organization with a similar mission. Doing so offers a number of advantages such as establishing credibility in the larger community and the ability to receive tax-deductible donations. The primary role of the non-profit should be to act as a partner to the community being built, providing support through fundraising and political negotiation. In terms of management, the role of the non-profit should be solely to provide oversight. The village should be self-managed, with the non-profit ensuring that the basic rules and agreements with the city are being upheld. Having residents of the village on the board of directors is critical for establishing representation and improving communication. The "Village Manual" included in Appendix B provides an organizational framework for this type of self-management with oversight.

OVE decided to go with a board-only organization based on the recommendation from members of Dignity Village to avoid their internal, membership-based organization. This structure better accommodates the role as an oversight organization. A membership structure—where the residents of the village are the members of the non-profit—allows residents to elect board members and change the bylaws of the organization. If the intent is to develop a transitional community, these members are then by definition intended to be in fluctuation. The board-only structure creates a firewall between the village and the non-profit. This establishes greater stability for the organization, which eases concerns of both the city and surrounding community. The structure also allows the non-profit to more easily take on multiple projects, each of which is then self-managed.

It is important to recognize, though, that this structure does pose the risk of the non-profit becoming more authoritative and vertically organized. If this approach is taken, it is critical to be selective in choosing board members so as to preserve values of autonomy and horizontal organization, and to not fall into the role of a traditional social service provider. The board of OVE is a truly collaborative effort that includes village residents, advocates, and community leaders. Although we recognize that the challenges and possibilities facing OVE will continue to evolve over the years, we believe that the OVE board embodies the kind of values and stakeholders that have shaped our successful strategic history, positioning us to provide guidance to the village—and future villages— in that same spirit well into our unpredictable future.

Chapter 17

Planning & Designing a Village

• • •

Once the issue is on the table, it is necessary for the advocacy group to better define the project they are envisioning. Here, the group progresses from advocating for an idea to planning and designing a pragmatic model that can meet the formal expectations of the city and appeal to the larger community. It is critical for the group to take the lead in determining how the place will be organized and what it will look like—specifically, demonstrating how the project can be an asset to the area rather than a band-aid. This chapter covers strategies for doing so through the planning and design of the village, again with specific reference to my experience with Opportunity Village.

Role of the Planner & Designer

The project should be focused as a citizen-driven initiative, but bringing in some professional expertise can be imperative to gaining political traction and developing an implementable plan. As an urban planner, I would like to focus in on that role, which I find to be a pivotal one in this type of development. Having an urban planner or architect with a similar ideology as the advocacy group can help navigate the formal planning and development process. In addition, a planner or architect with design experience can help define and illustrate the concept being proposed by the advocacy group.

It is commonly believed that a primary shortfall of the urban planning profession is its inability to effectively influence change; that too often lofty, well-intentioned plans are drafted only to gather dust on a shelf. In order to avoid this, the success of planning has come to rest on implementation. If a plan is not physically implemented it is commonly believed to have failed. But, in order to achieve implementation, planners usually feel the need to pay lip service to cultural norms of financial self-interest and auto-oriented development. As a result, the visions that aim to shape our future have been constrained by the status quo.

Instead, it is my belief that truly great plans are those that cause the public to see something that cannot exist, but undeniably *should* exist. When presented effectively, these concepts and ideas can enliven the public to demand change—to demand a better system that is more equitable, reasonable, and sustainable. To begin, one must make a clear argument founded on sound reason, to the point that the status quo seems entirely irrational. With the issue of homelessness, our existing methods and policies for dealing with the situation make this an easy argument. Unlike typical politics, exaggeration and fabrication are unnecessary—the facts are there, they just need to be presented in an effective manner to create a convincing vision for a better way forward.

So rather than conforming what we plan, maybe we should reconsider how we plan. Paul Davidoff's theory of "advoacy planning" offers an alternative paradigm in this regard. In his renowned 1965 article on the subject, Davidoff refutes the modern depiction of the planner as a "technician" that operates from a position of value neutrality. He argues that this is an unworkable role since the decision-making process is based on desired objectives. Since then, it has become more commonplace for planners to make their values known, but Davidoff takes this even further by declaring that the planner should then act as an advocate for those values.

In this sense, planners would represent various interest groups in the city, putting forth a multitude of plans that articulate the diverse interests of the community. This decentralized approach contrasts the prevalent norm of a centralized planning department that produces a single plan, which the public has a limited ability to react to. Instead, a variety of plans would be presented from different sources to better inform politicians and the public in the decision-making process. As Davidoff points out, "The right choice of action is always a matter of choice, never of fact."[133]

Placing advocacy planning within the context of this book, a planner could be responsible for representing a local tent city initiative to develop a plan that articulates their interests. Maybe they simply want a safe and legal place to be or maybe they have a more elaborate vision of developing a tiny house village. The planner would then advocate that plan to politicians and the public.

While this may seem like a fringe theory, it is actually supported by the profession's code of ethics. The American Institute of Certified Planners (AICP) obligates a planner to work "to expand choice and opportunity for all persons, recognizing a special responsibility to plan for the needs of the disadvantaged and to promote racial and economic integration," and to "urge the alteration of policies, institutions, and decisions that oppose such needs." Advocacy planning puts these ethics into action. The planner, trained to see the big picture, is uniquely positioned to be a valuable asset in addressing homelessness by providing long-term vision to an issue that is so often addressed with short-term, stop-gap measures.

Concept Plan

A well-crafted concept plan can help the project transcend the stigma of the "homeless camp" to the optimism of a "village." Illustrations of the concept being proposed can especially bring the project to life for a wider audience. But community cannot be created in isolation, so it is important to include a participatory design process. A design workshop is a good way to broaden your support network by allowing more of the community—both housed and unhoused—to provide input to the plan. Here, it is useful to find a planner or architect with similar values to help facilitate this pivotal stage of the project. Along with developing a better common understanding of what it is you are planning, the experience can forge new relationships that will carry the project forward.

Formulating a design program should be a primary goal in this part of the process. Before drawing any plans, it is first necessary to decide what should be included in the drawing. The design program establishes a list of physical elements necessary to support the group's goals. What activities and functions need to be accommodated on site to achieve those goals? How many people must they support? A planner or architect can help guide the discussion, offer important considerations, and provide technical assistance such as how much square footage is required to support a given activity. In the end, you should have a comprehensive list of site features with an approximate square footage and brief description of the use for each feature.

The design program provides others with a better understanding of what the actual physical building blocks of the village will be. Workshop participants can then use those building blocks to develop various design alternatives with a scaled model. Ultimately a single concept design should be selected that best illustrates the goals and program of the project. This is not necessarily the design that will be built, since the site may be hypothetical at this point, but it can provide valuable conceptual direction in the planning process. It will help guide your group internally as well as clarify your intent to the city by declaring the number and size of structures, parking spaces, and land area you are proposing. It may not meet all of the formal expectations, but it provides a starting point for the city to react to.

While the physical plan for the village is important to articulate, it is equally important to determine how the village will be organizationally structured and managed. How will the residents of the village be selected? How will it be governed? What will the residents contribute? At this stage, it is not important to answer every item in detail, but to have general answers to the basic questions that will be asked by both the city and the public. By combining this organizational information with the physical design details discussed above, you should have a well-rounded concept plan on which your project can stand. For reference, a concept plan for Opportunity Village has been included in Appendix A of this book.

Community Agreement

The community agreement is the cornerstone of a self-managed camp or village. This key document that all residents must sign and abide by sets the basic expectations for living in the community, similar to a tenant agreement. There are consequences for residents that break agreements that in some cases can result in eviction. These agreements often develop informally within an unsanctioned camp, and should be preserved when formalizing a camp. Along with setting a standard within, the agreement is also a concise way for informing the surrounding community of the positive culture that the village is trying to foster. In short, dispelling the common stereotypes of the "homeless camp."

The community agreement established during the proposal for Opportunity Village has been included on the opposite page. The five basic rules were borrowed from Dignity Village, which we felt had been tried and tested, and the agreements that follow were heavily influenced by what had been drafted during the local Occupy camp.

Building Community

The initial residents that the community is being planned for should be identified during the planning process. Ideally it would be from the beginning but this is not always feasible for various reasons. The community building process will vary significantly based upon local conditions. Is there already an existing, unsanctioned camp that you are planning for? Or are you planning a community from scratch? Maybe a camp eviction prompted the advocacy effort but the population is now dispersed?

Most sanctioned examples that have retained self-governance evolved from tent cities that self-organized—meaning they are built from pre-existing relationships, agreements, and policies. Opportunity Village is a rare exception. While the eviction of a camp prompted the model to be considered by the city, the unhoused population was widely dispersed by the event. Coming into the project, the lack of existing stakeholders was a major concern of mine, but in the end our group was able to resolve the issue. Consequently it provides an example for how to build the community of a Transitional Village model from scratch.

Opportunity Village | Community Agreement

Opportunity Village is a transitional micro-housing village that provides a safe and secure place to be for those currently without housing. It is a self-governing community that is based on five basic rules:

1) No violence to yourselves or others

2) No theft

3) No alcohol, illegal drugs, or drug paraphernalia

4) No persistent, disruptive behavior

5) Everyone must contribute to the operation and maintenance of the Village.

I will be a positive member of this community and contribute toward making it a safe, secure, clean, and pleasant place to live. Therefore I agree to the following:

◊ What I do will be based on love and respect for myself and others.

◊ I will not disrespect others based on ethnicity, religion, gender, sexual orientation, handicap, lifestyle choices, or economic status. We all have the right to expect dignity and opportunity.

◊ I will help make this a place where everyone feels safe and respected. For my own safety as well as the safety of others, I will not carry a weapon or act violently toward others or myself.

◊ Since stealing is one of the most upsetting things that can happen in our community, I will not steal and will make the members of the Village Council aware of any stealing I see. I will respect other people's property and community property and I expect other people to respect mine.

◊ I know that illegal drug and alcohol use can damage my community. I agree not to use illegal drugs or alcohol while residing in the Village.

◊ I will honor quiet hours from 10PM to 7AM so that others and myself can stay healthy and rested. I understand that no personal guests will be allowed during that time.

◊ I want to live in a clean, litter-free, comfortable space where I can bring friends, family, and other guests. Also, I know that many communities such as ours get closed down for "health and safety" reasons. I will keep the area in and around where I live clean and orderly, and not store any personal items outside of my building footprint or allocated storage space. I will help keep the community areas clean and will pick up after myself and my pet, if I have one, and keep my pet leashed at all times. I understand that only a limited number of pets will be allowed in the Village in order to maintain an orderly environment.

◊ I understand that in order to maintain a secure environment there will be a single point of entrance and exit that will be staffed 24/7, and that security shifts will be shared equally among Village residents.

◊ I know that it can take a lot of work to keep the Village a safe, clean and pleasant place to live. I agree to work at least 10 hours a week on the operation and maintenance of the Village. This includes serving on security teams, helping with kitchen duties, construction projects, maintenance and clean-up crews, helping plan activities, and other jobs that need to be shared by community members.

◊ I also know that there are financial costs to keep the Village running. I will support the goal of self-sufficiency by contributing each month either financially or through sweat equity by participating in micro-business opportunities or fundraising events.

◊ I will attend the weekly Village meetings, unless I have an acceptable reason for absence, in which case I will find out what went on by reading the meeting notes. I understand that decisions will be made through a majority vote, and that the Board of Directors of the non-profit reserves the right to override decisions made. I agree to abide by all decisions made.

◊ I affirm that I have completed the Background Check Form honestly along with all other application documents. I understand that if the background check reveals otherwise, I could be asked to leave immediately.

◊ I promise to keep all of these agreements, as well as others that are approved at Village meetings. If I violate any agreements, the members of the Village Council are authorized to ask me to leave temporarily, or, in serious or repeat cases, to leave permanently. I will do so peacefully and not return unless I am authorized to do so.

I know that Opportunity Village is a place where people value community and support each other. I will try to think of ways to make our community a better place to be. When I am concerned or upset with situations in the Village, I will bring these problems to the attention of the appropriate people so that we can work together to figure things out. I willingly sign these agreements that are a contract between Opportunity Village Eugene and me.

Signature:_____ Date:_____

Our community building process began in the church parking lot that hosted the first three Conestoga huts. The people housed there became involved in the planning of the project, and two of the three ended up becoming residents at the village. In a way, it provided an initial social experiment prior to the opening of the village. It turned out that one couple staying there was heavily using drugs, which came to light after an incident of domestic violence. This resulted in a deep and philosophical discussion by our board of directors that ultimately resulted in their eviction from the hut. It highlighted that the project we were planning would not always be pretty, and if we wanted to gain the respect of the public, we needed to follow through with the rules that we had set forth. It was an unpleasant experience, but a good one to have under our belt before the village opened.

Shortly thereafter we formed an application process and vetting committee. The application included a background check, skills inventory, and questionnaire. Applications were available to be picked up and returned at various locations around town. The vetting committee then reviewed the applications, and selected interviewees that seemed most apt for the village culture we were trying to create. In the end, we accepted the first fifteen people we interviewed. These folks established our "core group," and pre-village meetings began to be held twice a week in a church basement. This allowed the group to get to know one another and begin to make decisions on how the village would be run prior to opening.

We knew it was a pilot project and we wanted to establish a core group that would ensure its success. The meetings were facilitated by members from the non-profit, and the main purpose besides relationship building was to transfer the knowledge that had been developed thus far in the planning process to the residents that would eventually manage it. This ultimately led to the drafting of a village manual—a written explanation of how the village would be operated and maintained. These meetings occurred for around three months while we were simultaneously going through the public process required to legally open the site.

The Village Manual

Managing any large number of people can be a challenge, and adding a staff to do so is costly, both economically and socially in this context. In setting out to determine how a village should be managed, I have borrowed significantly from the effective forms of self-management and direct democracy that I found in my visits to various tent cities throughout the country.

The village manual consolidates these findings into a basic framework for operating and maintaining a self-managed village. If the community agreement is what holds the village together, the village manual is what keeps it running. It is based on the organizational structure that tends to develop organically in many self-organized tent cities, which can be a useful tool for advocate groups aiming to start a village without an existing community in place. The intent is to provide a very initial structure that a self-governing community can then amend and expand upon based on experience. Here, simplicity is crucial, since each rule has to be enforced. It is imperative to realize that you cannot preemptively plan for every possible situation that may arise, and even if you could, doing so would be undesirable since it would distort the autonomous character of this model. But having a basic operational manual to start from can ease the anxieties of all parties involved.

The manual for Opportunity Village has been provided for reference in Appendix B of this book. It is based on the establishment of a partner non-profit organization with a board-only organizational structure. The document was developed and refined during the initial core group meetings in the months prior to the village opening, and also incorporated the expectations and standards set by our operational agreement with the city. All new residents receive a manual and an existing resident serves as a "guide" to help orient them on the rules and expectations of the village.

The manual is updated quarterly to include amendments and addendums passed at village meetings. The edition included in this book incorporates revisions from the first two quarters of operation. Based upon on-the-ground experience, we found that some of our original policies were not being followed and instead replaced with more practical alternatives. While the manual has been updated since the edition included in this book, it has become increasingly specific to the community using it. The intent of including this early document is to provide a starting point for other communities that can then adapt it based upon their own preferences and experiences.

Working with the City and Neighbors

Since the village model diverges from conventional development, working with the city is not a simple or straightforward task. Planning and building departments are run by standards and regulations that inhibit this type of human-scale, citizen-driven development. But, by positioning the project as a low-cost initiative where the community is addressing a major problem at little cost to the city, you should be able to find some leeway to develop economically creative solutions that avoid traditional development procedures that inflate costs. Understandably, there will be certain standards that the municipality will hold you to, but they should be based on legitimate concerns for health and safety rather than simply upholding the status quo.

In working with the City of Eugene, I found that most staff supported the idea of the village model we were proposing, but we had to cooperate in order to find a formal resolution for legitimizing the project. The major piece here was that even though a site had been approved by city council, it required we first obtain a conditional use permit (CUP). Acquiring the CUP involved a lengthy public process, which can often make or break a project. But we were able to succeed on this front by getting ahead of the process.

To start, our organization preemptively introduced the project at a neighborhood association meeting. Following a presentation of what we were proposing for the site, a lengthy question and answer session ensued. It was a full house and many concerns were raised. Along with members of our board of directors, Mark Hubbell, a previous member of Portland's Right 2 Dream Too, also attended and was able to respond to questions with first hand experiences, which seemed to go a long way.

By the end of the meeting, the president of the neighborhood association asked if anyone remained opposed to the project, to which no hands were raised. The neighbors wanted to be updated on the progress of the project, so liaisons between our group and the neighborhood association were established. In addition, a liaison from the police department was identified, and we met individually with adjacent business owners to listen and respond to their specific concerns.

Following all this, as part of the CUP process, we were required to send public notice to occupants within 500 feet of the site and hold an official pre-application neighborhood meeting. But by this point, less than a handful of people showed up for the meeting, and again no opposition was raised. One attendee raised the point that the neighborhood had the lowest income per capita in the city, and that the people there may have been so open minded to the project precisely because they recognized being only one or two paychecks away from homelessness themselves.

The process also included pre-development meetings with city staff. A CUP deals with physical land use, and a lot of the application fields were not pertinent to the minimal amount of development that we were proposing. Instead, an operational agreement was drafted to be the primary binding agreement between the city and OVE. This is where submitting our own plan was advantageous. The city basically used our plan as a basis for the agreement, tweaked it to satisfy specific concerns, and added the necessary legal language.

Our building department was not comfortable with simply turning a blind-eye to the small structures we were proposing, but they worked with us to form a streamlined permitting process that reduced technical and financial burdens, yet still ensured structural integrity. We were able to get a flexible, modular design pre-approved that could then be replicated with a degree of variety. Insulation and permanent foundation standards were also reduced, which are commonly major hurdles to tiny houses. The building department interpreted the development as an "organizational campground" and we were held to similar regulations. Each unit had to be within a defined "camp site" with sites spaced at least ten feet apart.

Our work with both the neighborhood and city staff culminated in an official hearing that would decide whether the CUP would be approved or denied. A third party hearings official came in from Salem and anyone was granted the opportunity to speak in support or opposition of the project. Several parties spoke in support of the project including city staff, the neighborhood association president, and several of the core members that were waiting for a place to live. When it came time to voice opposition no one got up to speak. A member of the planning commission who had helped guide us through the process said it was the first time he had ever witnessed no opposition to a land use issue. It was also a unique situation in that the hearings official informed us that the CUP would be approved at the end of the meeting (they have up to two weeks to make a decision). At this point, we knew the village would soon be real and so turned our attention fully to building.

Chapter 18

Building a Village

• • •

And now for the fun part—the building of the village! To guide this process, I developed a "Village Building Catalog" to further define the physical building blocks of the village being proposed. The catalog compiled various builders and building styles that demonstrated simplicity, efficiency, transportability, and aesthetics. In an effort to involve a wide range of participants in the building process, the structures included were designed so that construction and assembly is simple and straightforward. This enabled the building of Opportunity Village to be a unique collaboration between skilled builders, village residents and applicants, and community volunteers. Additionally, the structures were designed to do the most with the least amount of materials—utilizing discounted or recycled materials when appropriate and reducing wasted. Since it was a pilot project, the structures included had to have the ability to be transported if necessary in order to accommodate flexibility in location. At the same time, they had to be aesthetic to gain political support, and to reduce the chance that neighbors or city officials would want to move them. A more detailed description of some of the proposed structures is covered in this chapter along with the patterns and illustrative plan that guided the building.

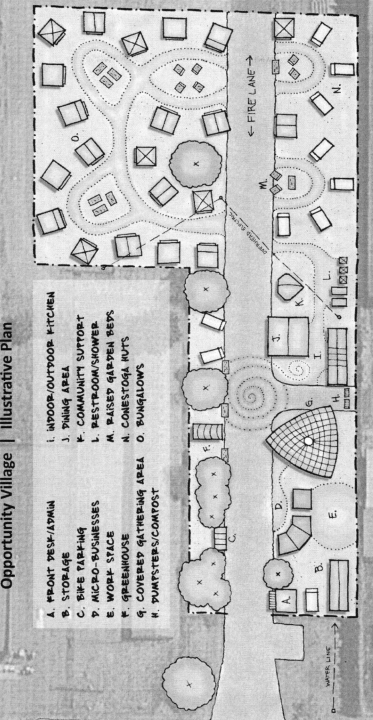

Opportunity Village | Illustrative Plan

A. FRONT DESK/ADMIN
B. STORAGE
C. BIKE PARKING
D. MICRO-BUSINESSES
E. WORK SPACE
F. GREENHOUSE
G. COVERED GATHERING AREA
H. DUMPSTERS/COMPOST
I. INDOOR/OUTDOOR KITCHEN
J. DINING AREA
K. COMMUNITY SUPPORT
L. RESTROOM/SHOWER
M. RAISED GARDEN BEDS
N. CONESTOGA HUTS
O. BUNGALOWS

N. GARFIELD STREET

← FIRE LANE →

WATER LINE

OVERHEAD ELECTRIC

N

10 10 10 FT

Illustrative Plan

Once a site is identified, the patterns and design program defined in the concept plan can be applied to fit the specific constraints of the site. An illustrative plan provides a graphic depiction of one of many possible designs within a given framework. While development is not tied to the illustrative plan, as is the case with a site plan, a preferred plan can provide a vision forward as the village grows. As lessons are learned with experience, the plan can then be adapted and updated.

I encourage trying to build this kind of flexibility into the design to preserve a degree of the organic growth found in the self-organized camps. This distinguishes the project from conventional development, where the design is set in stone before construction begins, and the entire development is constructed before any person ever inhabits it. The village model should be built gradually over time through piecemeal growth. This allows for greater participation and ownership from the people who live their, as well as a more authentic and interesting built environment.

Conestoga Huts

The six by ten foot Conestoga hut is a seriously economical shelter. It makes significant improvements upon the tent—most notably an insulated and lockable space—while minimizing the cost, skill, and labor required by a more conventional, four-walled structure. There are three components to the huts: 1) an insulated floor with and attached front porch, 2) two wood-framed, insulated walls in the front and back of the structure, and 3) cattle panel wiring that is curved to connect to the long ends of the floor. The wired roof frame is then covered with Mylar insulation followed by outdoor vinyl that is attached to the base of the structure.

When completed, the result is a structure that resembles the Conestoga wagons used during early American westward expansion. The components of the shelter can then be easily assembled or disassembled on site and transported with ease. This idea of moving and establishing one's own shelter draws a reference to the rugged individualism again linked with the Conestoga wagon.

A Village Pattern Language

A pattern is a preferable relationship among elements. To form a language, patterns can be combined in a number of different ways, similar to the words that compose a sentence. Christopher Alexander's *A Pattern Language* applies this concept to the building of towns and cities. Developing a language for the village you are planning can provide a non-technical vocabulary of design principles. Some patterns include:

Small Structures

Structures under 200 square feet in area and under 10 feet in average height will accommodate transportability and minimize permitting and material requirements.

Clustered Dwellings

Dwellings arranged facing a common center will encourage community cohesion and improve security by placing more eyes on private spaces.

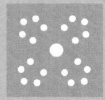

Degrees of Publicness

Each resident should have access to a small amount of private space, a larger amount of common space, as well as in between spaces to establish a balanced living environment.

By combining patterns with the building blocks presented in this chapter, an infinite number of development alternatives become possible within a defined framework. Rather than having a single, predetermined design for a development—commonly referred to as a site plan—a pattern language can guide the growth of the community as it evolves over time, resulting in a living environment that is once again reflective of the people who live there. Formulating a list of preferred patterns can help guide the development of an illustrative plan.

Erik de Buhr first built a primitive version of the hut for the local Occupy camp. The design was then developed to make these simple structures larger, more durable, and more aesthetic. The latter was key in gaining political support—people were captured by the "cuteness" of the huts, and they received seemingly unanimous support from city officials and the public.

The compact and transportable nature of the hut allows for providing very basic shelter to people in a variety of temporary settings. Furthermore, the simplicity of the structure does not require a building permit in Eugene. A non-profit organization, Community Supported Shelters, was formed to focus specifically on the building and siting of Conestoga huts, and more than two dozen have been placed throughout the city as part of our local car camping and rest stop programs. There are also nine huts at Opportunity Village, which serve as an entry portal to the micro-housing at the village. Often new residents will move into a hut, and when space becomes available, they will move into one of the structures covered next.

Backyard Bungalows

Much of Opportunity Village is comprised of tiny houses designed by Backyard Bungalows, a company started by Alex Daniell, Ted Drummond, and myself. The 64 and 80 square foot structures use a modular panelization technique that reduces waste and simplifies the assembly process so that more people can participate in the home building process. This allowed the village to be built during a series of volunteer events, similar to a traditional barn raising.

Modular panels for the floor, walls, and roof are first constructed at an off-site workshop space. These kits of between 11 and 19 panels—depending on size and roof style—are then stacked and loaded on a trailer to be transported to the site. Then, at the end of each month, we hosted a volunteer build event where the panels built during that month were assembled on site. The modular panelization allows for a quick and intuitive assembly process, similar to putting together a big puzzle. The framed structures can be completed in just a few hours with a handful of volunteers and someone that knows the process.

Conestoga Hut

Bungalow

Conic Shell

Plans were approved by the building department, and after the framed and sheathed structures were erected, a building inspection was scheduled with the city's building department. Once approved for occupancy, residents were free to finish and personalize the bungalows—adding features like front porches, interior furniture, insulation, murals, and gardens. The process allows for variation among the homes and encourages piecemeal growth. As initial residents move out, new residents move in that adapt and build upon the existing space.

The bungalows are also designed with transportability in mind. This was due to the temporary nature of the pilot project, but also with the intention that—as the name suggests—they could be placed in someone's backyard. With a more stable site, additional panels can be added to make a larger living space.

Conic Shells

The Conic Shell, a design by Chuck Henderson, is a stand-alone structure that can be used for a variety of uses including housing or common spaces. Based on the intrinsic strength of intersecting cones, and made entirely of quarter-inch plywood or oriented strand board that is bolted together, the Conic is a continuously curved structure that uses minimal materials to achieve maximum strength.

The shape creates an interior space that is both compact and spacious. The interior volume is two-thirds the volume of a conventional structure and can therefore be heated with minimal energy. And with an interior height of nine feet, the structure provides a comfortable living space with the potential for storage along the top ridge. Insulation can be installed between the exterior shell and a fabric interior finish.

The original design by Chuck—based in Point Arena, California—is sloped to sit on a foundation at ground level. However, a local builder here in Eugene known as Finn Po adapted the design to sit on a raised floor, reminiscent of his earlier Icosa hut structures. This hybrid model is better suited for the wet climate in the Pacific Northwest. While the original plan for Opportunity Village called for a handful of Conic Shells, in the end they were not pursued due to the engineering challenges required by the permitting process.

Common Facilities

A defining aspect of the village model is that the micro-housing is supported by common facilities. Sharing these resources keeps costs low, encourages social interaction, and reduces environmental impact. The primary common facilities constructed at Opportunity Village are identified below and pictured on the following page.

◊ Gathering Space: Determining a gathering space that was both large enough to accommodate 30 to 45 people yet still able to be relocated if necessary was no easy task. At first we were between a very temporary military-style tent and a more permanent wood-framed structure. However, we eventually found an ideal balance with a 30 foot wide yurt heated with a pellet stove. These historically nomadic structures are both moveable yet durable and spacious. The yurt comfortably accommodates the whole village year-round for weekly meetings, community events, and a general day-to-day common space.

◊ Bathroom: The "micro-BathHouse" includes a shower room, two restrooms with a flush toilet and sink, and a laundry room—all in just 112 square feet! The plumbing for the structure was built into the floor so that it can be disconnected at a single point and transported if necessary. Early on at Opportunity Village, portable toilets were rented and residents had to go off-site for showers and laundry, so the construction of this compact facility dramatically improved the quality of life at the village.

◊ Kitchen: The "LongHouse" is a combination of two or more bun-galows connected by a covered area. The idea here was to pursue a barbeque-style cooking area where food can be stored and prepared indoors and cooked outdoors in order to avoid stringent require-ments around commercial kitchens. At Opportunity Village this arrangement includes one structure as a food pantry and the other is wired to include a sink, refrigerator, and microwaves. In between the two, there is a covered deck with propane-fueled stoves and a very efficient wood-burning stove donated by InStove.

Gathering Space

Bathroom and Laundry Room

Common Kitchen

What You Can Do

• • •

The vision presented in this book is not only possible—it's happening. These initial projects have blazed a trail, and it is up to you to make it a well traveled one. Here are some ways that you can contribute to this budding movement:

◊ Spread the word: Much like the bottom-up initiatives that have just been presented, this book has been published independently. So it will take a grassroots movement to spread the word about this new housing paradigm. You could play a significant role in this. Please consider informing your networks about this book and the possibilities it brings to light. At www.thevillagecollaborative.net you can:

  • Order multiple copies at a reduced price to distribute to friends, colleagues, neighbors or city officials

  • Inquire about a presentation or workshop in your area

  • Find additional resources related to the content of this book

◊ Conduct outreach: Visit local tent cities and find out what the needs and desires are in your area. If you are living in a tent city, visit other camps and connect with advocates to build a network.

◊ <u>Form an advocacy group:</u> Find others with a similar interest and begin meeting regularly to plan a village in your area—or join an existing initiative with a similar mission. If further direction is needed, the Village Collaborative can provide consulting advice or services.

◊ <u>Learn more and join the conversation:</u> Visit the Tent City Urbanism blog at www.tentcityurbanism.com for more information on the issues and projects presented in this book. Here you can also:

- Subscribe to receive updates through e-mail

- Join the conversation by posting to our forum—a place to share stories, ask questions, introduce projects, and learn from the experiences of others on a similar journey

- Submit a guest post for the blog

◊ <u>Build a tiny house prototype:</u> Advance the conversation in your area by building a tiny house prototype. You can find free plans at www.backyardbungalows.net for the modular bungalows built at Opportunity Village.

◊ <u>Contribute to an existing organization:</u> Consider contributing skills, materials, or money to one of the non-profit organizations in this book. To contribute to Opportunity village Eugene, an organization that puts many of the ideas within this book into action, please visit www.opportunityvillageeugene.org for more information.

◊ <u>Join the team:</u> Have an idea for a service that you could provide that would help catalyze village projects in other areas? If so, please inquire about joining the Village Collaborative.

Appendix A | **Opportunity Village Concept Plan**

Organizational Structure

◊ <u>Board of Directors:</u> Opportunity Village Eugene (OVE) is a non-profit organization with a Board of Directors that includes diverse experience and established community leaders.

◊ <u>Steering Committee:</u> In addition to the Board of Directors, a Steering Committee of at least ten regular members meets weekly to discuss and plan the project.

◊ <u>Advisory Board:</u> Advisors with specific professional expertise have signed on to consult the project and will provide technical assistance, training, and other support as needed.

◊ <u>Liability Insurance:</u> Liability coverage will be obtained from Gales Creek, which insures the Oregon Country Fair and Portland's Dignity Village.

Pilot Project

OVE is proposing a pilot project for 30 adults on suitable land controlled by the city that has access to public utilities, access to public transportation (within ¼ mile), borders that can be controlled, and at least one acre in area. OVE will construct simple "micro-houses" that are secure, lockable, and insulated. The Village will be self-governed with oversight provided by the Board of Directors. The basic, non-negotiable rules will include: 1) No violence to yourselves or others, 2) no theft, 3) no alcohol, illegal drugs, or drug paraphernalia, 4) No persistent, disruptive behavior, and 5) Everyone must contribute to the operation and maintenance of the Village.

To the extent possible, residents will be involved in the building process so that they may earn "sweat equity" toward the value of their shelter. We are partnering with local builders that are developing transportable and economical structures. Along with individual homes, the Village will include a kitchen and dining area, bathrooms with showers, a gathering space for meetings, and opportunities for gardening and micro-business initiatives.

Village Management Program

◊ Application and Intake Process: All applicants will complete the Village application and intake documents, which will include a background check form, medical questionnaire, application and intake questionnaire, and skills inventory. To begin the pilot project, the non-profit organization will select a core group of around ten to fifteen people through a vetting process based on relationship building. Once the core group is established, they will then conduct the process for gradually accepting new residents, much like existing self-governing models in Portland and Seattle.

◊ Community Agreement: If the applicant is found to be a good fit for the Village, they must then sign the Community Agreement that states expected behaviors and consequences for violations. An initial agreement will be established by the non-profit organization for the start of the pilot project, but residents will then have the right to amend the agreement. The Board of Directors of the non-profit organization will provide oversight and retains the right to override any amendment to the agreement.

◊ Village Meetings: Based on existing examples in Portland and Seattle, the community will be self-governed through regular weekly meetings that all residents are expected to attend. At this time residents will make decisions through majority vote about how the community is organized within the framework of the aforementioned basic rules. Specific roles will be identified and filled in order to maintain a safe and sanitary environment.

◊ Village Council: During the meetings, a small group of residents will be elected to the Village Council for a set period of time. These individuals will be responsible for monitoring the Village and taking immediate action with regard to any violations of the Community Agreement.

◊ Volunteers: Support and oversight from trained volunteers is an important piece for the initial stages of the Village, and will be utilized as necessary. Over time, the need for volunteer involvement will likely decrease as the residents themselves will take on more responsibility.

◊ Security: The Village will have a single, secure point of entry and exit that will be staffed by residents or trained volunteers. Every resident will share security duties at the gate. All visitors will be required to register at the front gate and be escorted by a resident. Those on duty will also patrol the immediate area outside of the gate to maintain a safe surrounding environment. The front gate will be locked from 12am-8am. The person on security shift during this time may sleep on a cot in the front office. Residents returning late or leaving early can make arrangements with the person on the overnight shift. The Eugene Police Department (EPD) will be welcome to patrol Opportunity Village as they would any other neighborhood in Eugene. A liaison from EPD to OVE has already been identified. In a situation in which the Village Council is unable to gain cooperation of a resident, the police will be called for assistance.

◊ Food: A covered barbecue-style cooking area will allow residents and volunteers to prepare hot meals on site, and may be supported by a mobile food cart. An adjacent pantry will provide food storage for residents and planned group meals, which will be managed by a resident designated as a kitchen manager. Any meals prepared by outside organization will follow the criteria set by the Benevolent Meal Site Information Guide set by the Oregon Health Authority. The establishment of a "local foodshed" will also be encouraged in which residents of the Village and members of the surrounding community come together to share locally grown produce.

◊ <u>Storage:</u> Due to the compact size of the dwelling units, resident will be allowed to bring only a minimal amount of possessions on site. To maintain a safe and orderly environment, personal items will not be stored outside of the footprint of one's dwelling.

◊ <u>Pets:</u> A limited number of pets will be allowed in the Village. This will be determined on a case-by-case basis to uphold a safe and sanitary environment.

◊ <u>Skill Building:</u> The non-profit organization will encourage resident skill building in a variety of ways. Cooking, gardening, and construction will be practical skills emphasized by the village model. In addition, the Village will strive to host a variety of educational classes and workshops for both residents and members of the larger community.

◊ <u>Financial Costs:</u> OVE will lease land from the City for a nominal fee. The non-profit will also maintain a fundraising campaign that actively seeks grants and donations to cover capital and operating costs. Resident contribution to the operating costs of the Village will be encouraged either from their own income or through micro-business opportunities that will be developed in which residents provide goods or services in order to raise money. A primary goal is for the Village to be self-sustaining. The capital budget will be kept small by the ecological philosophy of the Village.

◊ <u>Evaluation:</u> Records will be kept to determine where residents are coming from, where they go when they leave, whether new sources of income or employment have been generated, as well as general population demographics and other data. This evaluation will provide information on which aspects of the pilot project are most effective.

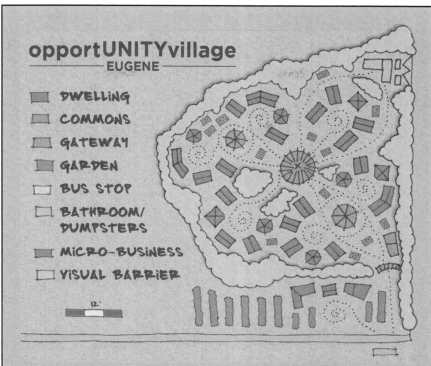

Early concept plan for Opportunity Village

Ground-level rendering of concept plan

Village Design Program

◊ <u>Village Gateway</u>: An appropriately designed and crafted landmark that will introduce residents and visitors to the Village.

◊ <u>Front Desk (80sf)</u>: Located just inside the Village Gateway and staffed by residents and/or trained volunteers to provide information to visitors and maintain a safe environment within. This multi-purpose structure will support the day-to-day operation of the Village.

◊ <u>Covered Bicycle Parking</u>: Secure and covered bicycle parking area near the front gate.

◊ <u>Dwellings (60-80sf)</u>: Micro-housing with lockable doors and front porches. The pilot project will be limited to no more than 30 dwellings that will include "bungalows" and "huts."

◊ <u>Indoor/Outdoor Kitchen (320sf)</u>: Two enclosed spaces—one for storage and one wired and plumbed—connected by a covered "barbecue-style" cooking area with propane-fueled stoves.

◊ <u>Gathering Area (750sf)</u>: An enclosed and heated area for meetings and events that will comfortably accommodate at least 40 people. This space will also include electrical outlets and act as a central charging station for residents.

◊ <u>Covered Gathering Area (400sf)</u>: A covered canopy for outdoor gatherings and activities.

◊ <u>Restrooms & Laundry Complex (112sf)</u>: Two toilets (one handicapped accessible) with sinks, one shower, and a washer/dryer unit.

◊ <u>Notional Community Support (120sf)</u>: A flexible structure that can support additional uses desired by residents such as a spiritual sanctuary or village library.

◊ <u>Donations & Tool Storage (200sf)</u>: A space to accommodate incoming donations to be organized for use and distribution. These items will be part of the local village economy.

◊ <u>Micro-Businesses</u>: Spaces to accommodate independent work areas and allow residents to sell or trade their goods and services to economically support the Village.

◊ <u>Greenhouse</u>: A space for growing certain crops year round. Additional uses may also be pursued in this area such as aquaponic systems, bee keeping, chicken coops, or composting.

◊ <u>Raised Garden Beds</u>: Simple raised garden beds of varying sizes will provide organic food, an aesthetically pleasant environment, and the opportunity to invest in one's immediate surroundings.

◊ <u>Garbage & Recycling</u>: Clustered near the common area for ease of access by residents and service trucks.

◊ <u>Path Network</u>: A defined path network that connects the various structures of the Village and reduces mud during the wet season.

◊ <u>Parking/Loading Area</u>: Short-term parking will be provided just outside the front gate for visitors and loading/unloading. There will be no long-term resident parking on site and the primary means of resident transportation is expected to be by bicycle or bus. The non-profit organization will provide residents with bus passes.

Appendix B | **Village Manual**

Types of Membership

◊ <u>Villager:</u> An individual who has been accepted as a member of the community. New villagers undergo a two week training period supported by an existing villager, known as a village guide. The new villager is a non-voting member during this time period.

◊ <u>Village Council Member:</u> 5 or 7 residents elected to have additional responsibility in managing the Village. A more detailed description of this role can be found under Village Governance.

◊ <u>Village Volunteer:</u> A non-villager or prior villager who is trained to assist in the operation and maintenance of the Village. They must be familiar with the Community Agreement and Village Manual.

◊ <u>Board of Directors:</u> Elected or appointed individuals who oversee the activities of the non-profit organization.

Agreements

◊ <u>Community Agreement:</u> The internal agreement that outlines expectations and acceptable conduct for villagers.

◊ <u>Operational Agreement:</u> The formal agreement between the non-profit organization and the City that regulates what the Village can and can't do.

Village Governance

Self-governance is a core value of the Village. This means that the success of the Village rests on the participation of those who live here. There are three governing groups for making decisions related to the management of the Village. They are:

1) Weekly Village Meeting (All Residents)

Every _____ at _____ a mandatory weekly meeting will be held. Attendance is mandatory for all residents. Issues related to the organization of the Village will be discussed and voted on at this time. Specific roles will be identified and filled in order to maintain a safe and sanitary environment. The following applies to the mandatory meeting:

◊ Advanced notice with documentation must be provided to the front desk for excused absences (i.e. work, school, medical), which must be approved by Village Council.

◊ Excused absences may vote on policy issues prior to the meeting through absentee ballot.

◊ A quorum is established when over 50% of residents are present.

◊ Any decisions made at the weekly meeting must comply with the existing Community Agreement, Village Manual, and Operational Agreement.

◊ Amendments to the Community Agreement and Village Manual may be proposed at the meeting and require a majority vote to pass.

◊ Amendments to the Community Agreement and Village Manual will be reviewed and approved by the Board of Directors before taking effect.

◊ Expulsion from the Village may be appealed at the weekly meeting, and is decided upon by a majority vote of the Village.

2) Village Council (Elected Residents)

Elections are held during the weekly meeting to maintain a Village Council of 5 or 7 residents. To become a council member, a villager must be nominated by another resident. A majority vote of villagers present then decides which nominees are elected. The elected term is two months. Council members may serve consecutive terms if they are nominated and receive 2/3 majority vote. Elections are to be staggered so that the entire council does not change at once.

The role of the Village Council is to uphold orderly management of the Village. The council is not meant to have greater power than any other villager. Villagers elected to the council are simply given the task of responding to incidents when the Community Agreement is broken, and enacting the appropriate level of intervention as specified within this manual. A primary responsibility of the council is to act between meetings when urgent situations arise. There is to be a designated "councilor of the day" as a point of contact.

For the issues addressed within this manual, it is the responsibility of the Village Council to ensure that the appropriate level of intervention is being enforced. A council member may be removed from their position for violating this duty through a majority vote at a weekly meeting. When an incident occurs that is not described in this manual, it is up to the council to determine the appropriate level of intervention.

All Village Council decisions are potentially subject to review by the entire village at a weekly meeting. In this way, service on the council is much like any other form of contribution to the operation and maintenance of the Village. The Village Council is to hold at least two regular meetings per week. During this time council members:

1) Set the agenda for the next weekly meeting (any villager can propose items)

2) Review incident reports and listen to appeals

3) Review front desk log and make sure everyone is completing their host shifts

4) Deal with other issues relevant to maintaining orderly operation of the Village

Impromptu Village Council meetings may also be necessary to address urgent situations. The quorum for holding a Village Council meeting is to have at least 50% of members present, but an attempt should be made to notify all council members. Members of the Board of Directors may also attend these meetings, but may not vote.

3) Board of Directors (Non-profit Organization)

The main governing role of the Board of Directors is to provide oversight. The purpose of this is to ensure that the Community Agreement and Village Manual are being upheld. In cases where the Village is not in compliance, and the Village Council has not taken action, the Board of Directors may step in to take action at its discretion.

The Board of Directors is also responsible for ensuring that financial, legal, administrative, safety, and sanitation matters are being properly managed. Interface between the Village and the Board will occur through the following:

◊ Resident Board Members: There will be at least two villagers appointed to the Board for six month terms. Resident board members are appointed by the Board of Directors and may not simultaneously serve on the Village Council.

◊ Village Council Liaison: One Village Council member will be appointed monthly by the council to attend board meetings, serving as a liaison between the council and the Board of Directors.

Village Security Plan

The front desk is the only gateway in and out of the Village and shall remain secure. Staffing the front desk is one of the most important duties at Opportunity Village. This will be a mandatory service of all villagers.

The front desk is to be staffed by at least two trained individuals during open hours (8am-10pm). At least one person must be a villager. The second may be a villagers or a village volunteer. The primary purpose of this duty is to be the "eyes and ears" of the Village during your shift. Staffing the front desk involves the following duties:

1) Register visitors and locate a villager to accompany the visitor

2) Document any disruption to normal operations in the log book

3) Inner perimeter checks of the site

4) Notify Village Council when you witness a rule break

The gate will be locked between 12am-8am. During this time, one person is to spend the night at the front desk in case assistance is needed at the gate. In the case of an incident, the resident on duty should write an incident report and alert a council members.

Weapons are not allowed at the Village. Weapons are defined as firearms, knives (other than small pocket knives with 4" blade or less or those used for cooking), explosives of any type, clubs, or other striking implements. Chemicals such as mace or pepper spray must be checked at the front desk.

There are three stages of response for maintaining a secure and orderly environment at the Village. Stage 1 is the least severe and most common type of response. Stage 3 is the most severe and least common type of response.

Stage 1: Village Council

Village Council members are responsible for maintaining order when urgent situations arise. For a full description of this duty see the Intervention Action Plan.

Stage 2: Intermediary Security Agency

When Village Council members are unable to gain the cooperation of a disruptive resident, they are to contact the intermediary security agency. A contract enables the security agency to act on behalf of the Village in order to gain control of the situation. The phone number for the security agency is listed at the front desk.

Stage 3: Eugene Police Department

The Eugene Police Department (EPD) is welcome to patrol the Village as they would any other neighborhood in Eugene. In cases where the law is being broken and residents or the security agency are unable to gain cooperation of the offender, the police department will be contacted. The previous two stages of response are to be tried first if appropriate. Contact the Eugene Police Department when a person crime is committed or is in progress, or upon a victim's request. Villagers may resolve lower level crimes such as petty theft and minor criminal mischief.

Intervention Action Plan

◊ When a complaint that is not technically a rule break is cause for concern to members of the Village, the Village Council will meet with said villager and discuss a plan of action to curtail the behavior. We hope that early intervention will help prevent further and more severe action.

◊ In cases of a complaint by one villager against another when the complaint is not a clear rule break, members of the Village Council or a third party mediator should meet with the complainant and the alleged offender to discuss the issue and reach a resolution that is agreeable to both parties.

◊ When a rule break occurs, any villager may write an incident report. The Village Council is then responsible for verifying that the level of intervention is appropriate and notifying the alleged offender. From there, the alleged offender has three options:

1) Accept the incident report with the proposed level of intervention

2) Appeal the incident report at the next council meeting, in which case the level of intervention requires the vote of a majority of council members

3) If the alleged offender still feels that the action is unjust they may appeal to the weekly meeting in which case a majority vote will either uphold or revise the decision

◊ Minor rule violations (i.e. missed host shift, missed weekly meeting, etc.) result in 4 levels of intervention:

Level 1 — Verbal Warning

Level 2 — Written Warning

Level 3 — 48 hour suspension from Village

Level 4 — Expulsion from Village

◊ Minor rule violations will be tracked for a 3 month rolling period.

◊ Villagers reserve the right to work off minor rule violations by contributing extra hours towards the operation and maintenance of the Village. Missed host shifts may be made up by working twice the number of hours missed. The Village Council will designate requirements for other minor rule violations.

◊ More severe rule violations may require action at a heightened level of intervention even though the rule violation may be a first offense. The Village Council will deal with these rule violations on a case-by-case basis unless defined in this manual.

◊ For incidents resulting in suspension or expulsion, the offender should be given a chance to appeal before taking their leave—unless the Village Council considers the behavior to be a threat to the Village.

◊ Villagers may appeal their expulsion from the Village at the weekly meeting, which may include actions for addressing the problematic behavior that caused their expulsion.

Food Storage Policy

Fair sharing of resources is critical to the well-being of the Village. Hoarding or inequitable division of resources is unhealthy. Additionally, the Village is vulnerable to food stealth by dogs, cats, rodents and other animals. Rodents themselves provide a health hazard and we must discourage their presence by not having food available to attract them. Consequently, the following Food Storage Policies have been adopted at the Village:

◊ All community food that enters the Village as a donation must be stored in the community food pantry in an appropriate sealed container. No donated food may be taken to an individual residence. All community food must be eaten in community areas.

◊ Non-perishable food purchased by the villagers with their own resources may be stored in rodent and insect resistant containers in their residence.

◊ A limited amount of perishable food may be stored in the community refrigerator if it is labeled with a name and date. Items in the refrigerator without a label immediately belong to "everyone." No perishable food may be stored in an individual residence.

◊ All food should be prepared in community areas.

◊ It is important, if one eats in their residence, to immediately wipe or sweep up any crumbs for the prevention of rodent infestation.

◊ Any villager who fails to store food properly in their unit may be ruled no longer able to have food in their unit.

Alcohol, Drug, and Paraphernalia Policy

◊ Possession of alcohol: 48 hour expulsion (enrollment in an AA program or random breathalyzer testing may also be required if Village Council deems necessary).

◊ Possession of marijuana or marijuana paraphernalia (including pipes made from other items: cans, vegetables, bottles, etc.): 48 hour expulsion.

◊ Other illegal drugs or drug paraphernalia, including needles (without medical prescription), pipes (used for anything other then tobacco or marijuana), and spoons that have been used for "cooking" drugs: permanent expulsion.

◊ Any other items suspected to have been used for drug related purposes will be dealt with on a case-by-case basis by the Village Council.

Abandonment Policy

Villagers who have been continuously absent from the Village and have made no effort to remain in contact for a period of 4 days have abandoned their dwelling. Said persons would no longer be a villager and their possessions would be removed from their previous dwelling immediately upon the dwelling being declared abandoned. They would then have a period of 30 days to retrieve their possessions after which time those items would be disposed of at Village discretion.

Exceptions will be made for residents who are unable to contact the Village due to extenuating circumstances such as jail, hospital, etc. Abandonment will not be considered for those villagers who wish to spend time away from the Village for personal reasons provided they inform the Village Council and make arrangements to cover their front desk host hours when possible. In the case of emergencies, exceptions will be made for those unable to make arrangements to cover their host hours.

Endnotes

1. National Alliance to End Homelessness, "The State of Homelessness in America," 10 (2013).

2. U.S. Conference of Mayors, "2012 Survey on Hunger and Homelessness," 2-3 (2012).

3. Shaila Dewan, "In Many Cities, Rent Is Rising Out of Reach of Middle Class," *The New York Times,* April 14, 2014.

4. See YouTube video: "St. Petersburg Police Cutting Up Homeless Tents," uploaded on 29 July 2007.

5. Harpo Productions, "Inside a tent city: a Lisa Ling exclusive," In *The Oprah Winfrey Show,* February 25, 2009.

6. Justin Sullivan, "From boom times to tent city," *MSNBC,* 2009, available at http://www.msnbc.msn.com/id/29528182/displaymode/1107/s/2/

7. Sasha Abramsky, "Tent cities don't tell poverty's full story," *The Guardian,* April 3, 2009.

8. Ibid.

9. Paul Thompson, "The credit crunch tent city which has returned to haunt America." *Daily Mail,* March 6, 2009.

10. National Coalition for the Homeless, "Tent cities in America: pacific coast report," 6 (2010).

11. Ibid, 8-9.

12. Ibid, 36.

13. Ibid, 39.

14. Katherine A. Longley, "Governing Homelessness: The Politics of Tent Cities in the U.S.," The John W. McCormack Graduate School of Policy Studies, 2-4 (2006).

15. Dale Maharidge, *The Last Great American Hobo,* (New York: Prima Publishing, 1993), 33.

16. Mark Lakeman, "A Concise History of the Grid," (1998).

17. Lewis Mumford, *Sticks & Stones: a study of American architecture and civilization,* (New York: Dover, 1955), 35-37.

18. Lakeman, "Concise History of the Grid," 14-17.

19. Charles Hoch and Robert Slayton, *New Homeless and Old*, (Philidelphia: Temple University Press, 1989), 52.

20. Ibid, 62.

21. Alan Durning, *Unlocking Home: Three Keys to Affordable Communities*, (Seattle: Sightline Institute, 2013).

22. Ibid.

23. Neil Smith, *The New Urban Frontier: gentrification and the revanchist city*, (New York: Routlege Press, 1996), 3-27.

24. For example see: "Downtown Cincinnati boutique hotel might replace low-income flats" *Cincinnati Business Courier*, September 28, 2009.

25. Smith, *New Urban Frontier*, 9.

26. Don Mitchell, *The Right to the City: social justice and the fight for public space*, (New York: Guilford Press, 2003), 161-190.

27. George L. Kelling and James Q. Wilson, "Broken Windows: The police and neighborhood safety, " *The Atlantic*, March 1, 1982.

28. Eric Lipton, "Computers to track quality of life crime, Giuliani says," *The New York Times*, November 15, 2000.

29. Steven D. Levitt and Stephen J. Dubner, *Freakonomics: a rogue economist explores the hidden side of everything*, (New York: William Morrow, 2005), 129.

30. Ibid, 129.

31. Lewin Group, "The Costs of Serving Homeless Individuals in Nine Cities," (2004).

32. Central Florida Commission on Homelessness, "The Cost of Long-Term Homelessness in Central Florida," (2014).

33. "25 IN PARK SHANTIES POLITELY ARRESTED; 'Hoover Valley' Colony in Old Reservoir Raided as Hamlet Is Deemed Health Hazard. ONE SHACK WAS 'RADIO CITY' There Jobless Squatters Gathered for Broadcasts -- Other Homes Showed Ingenuity of Builders.," *The New York Times*, September 22, 1932.

34. Jane Jacobs, *The Death and Life of Great American Cities*, (New York: Random House, 1961), 7.

35. John Groth and Eric Corjin, "Reclaiming urbanity: indeterminate spaces, informal actors and urban agenda setting," *Urban Studies*, 42, no. 3 (2005): 504.

36. Ibid, 505.

37. David Graeber, "Occupy Wall Street's anarchist roots," *Aljazeera*, November 13, 2011.

38. Erika Niedowski, "Occupy Wall Street Protesters Prepare for Winter Weather," *The Huffington Post*, October 29, 2011.

39. Smith, *New Urban Frontier*, 230-231.

40. Ibid, 231.

41. Ibid, 232.

42. Terence Chea, "Tiny house movement thrives after real estate bust," *USA Today*, November 29, 2010.

43. National Association of Home Builders, "Housing Facts, Figures and Trends," (2006), available at: http://www.soflo.fau.edu/report/NAH-BhousingfactsMarch2006.pdf

44. U.S. Census "Median and Average Square Feet of Floor Area in New Single-Family Houses Completed by Location," (2012), available at: http://www.census.gov/const/C25Ann/sftotalmedavgsqft.pdf

45. U.S. Department of Housing and Urban Development, "2011 Housing Profile: United States: American Housing Survey Factsheets," (2013), available at: http://www.census.gov/prod/2013pubs/ahs11-1.pdf

46. U.S. Green Building Council, "Buildings and Climate Change," available at: http://www.documents.dgs.ca.gov/dgs/pio/facts/LA%20workshop/climate.pdf

47. Ibid.

48. For example see: "In U.S. building industry, is it too easy to be green?," *USA Today*, June 13, 2013.

49. Jordan Palmeri, "Small Homes: Benefits, Trends and Policies," Oregon Department of Environmental Quality, 2010, available at: http://www.deq.state.or.us/lq/sw/wasteprevention/presentations.htm

50. Ken Kern, Ted Kogon, Rob Thallon, *The Owner-Builder and The Code: Politics of building your home*, (Oakhurst, CA: Owner-Builder Publications, 1976), 4-5.

51. Ibid, 15.

52. Jay Shafer, *The Tumbleweed DIY Book of Backyard Sheds & Tiny Houses*, (East Petersburg, PA: Fox Chapel, 2012), 15.

53. Michael Tortorello, "Small World, Big Idea," *The New York Times*, February 19, 2014.

54. Christopher Alexander, *A Timeless Way of Building*, (New York: Oxford University Press, 1979), 223-242.

55. Carrie Antlfinger, "Tiny Houses Help Address Nation's Homeless Problem," *Associated Press*, February 26, 2014.

56. Erika Lundahl, "Tiny Houses for the Homeless: An Affordable Solution Catches On," *Yes!*, February 20, 2014.

57. Ibid.

58. Dean Mosiman, "Madison Plan Commission approves 'tiny houses,'" *Wisonsin State Journal*, April 29, 2014.

59. Kathryn McCamant and Chuck Durrett, *Creating Cohousing: Building Sustainable Communities*, (Gabriola Island, BC: New Society Publishers, 2011), 277.

60. Ibid, 248-249.

61. Linda Joseph and Albert Bates, "What is an Ecovillage?", *Communities*, 2003, 17.

62. Bill McKibben, *Eaarth: Making a Life on a Tough New Plenet*, (New York: Times Books, 2010), 133.

63. Robert D. Putnam, *Bowling Alone: The Collapse and Revival of America*, (New York: Simon & Schuster, 2001).

64. Bill Mollison, *Permaculture: a designer's manual*, (Tyalgum, Australia: Tagari Publications, 1988), 519.

65. Caleb Poirier, Interview by author, August 11, 2010.

66. Caleb Poirier, Interview by author, June 29, 2010.

67. Danielle, Interview by author, June 29, 2010.

68. National Coalition for the Homeless "Hate Crimes Against the Homeless: America's growing tide of violence," (2010).

69. Lakeman, "Concise History of the Grid," 4.

70. Jacobs, *Death and Life of Great American Cities*, 35.

71. Christopher Alexander, *A New Theory of Urban Design*, (New York: Oxford University Press, 1987), 22.

72. Pete Cunningham, "Crowd supports Camp Take Notice as neighbors of Ann Arbor tent city circulate petition for eviction," *Ann Arbor News*, May 24, 2012.

73. Ryan J. Stanton, "State erects 8-foot fence to keep homeless from returning to Camp Take Notice site," *Ann Arbor News*, June 20, 2012.

74. Kyle Feldscher, "'Slow moving' process to find homes for former Camp Take Notice residents solidifies supporters' resolve to reopen camp," *Ann Arbor News*, August 5, 2012.

75. Doug Sanders, Interview by author, July 6, 2010.

76. City of Seattle, "History of Tent Cities in King County," available at http://www.seattle.gov/council/licata/homelessness/attachments/history.pdf

77. "Tent Cities in America," 18-24.

78. "SHARE/WHEEL and El Centro de la Raza v. the City of Seattle et al. Consent Decree," Municipal Research and Services Center of Washington, March 13, 2002, available at http://www.mrsc.org/govdocs/S42consent.pdf

79. Abhi Raghunathan, "Homeless fight back with high teach." *Tampa Bay Times*, February 2, 2007.

80. Rick Baker, *The Seamless City: A conservative mayor's approach to urban revitalization that can work anywhere*, (Washington, DC: Regnery Publishing, 2011), 169.

81. Ibid, 170-172.

82. Ibid, 172.

83. Steve Thompson and Rod Challenger, "St Petersburg Police Slash Tents of the Homeless," *Tampa Tribune*, January 20, 2007.

84. "Tent City in St. Petersburg, FL for the Homeless," St. Pete for Peace, available at: http://stpeteforpeace.org/tentcitypage2.html

85. "Tent city residents are a part of the community," *Tampa Bay Times*, January 10, 2007.

86. "Tent City," St. Pete for Peace.

87. Abhi Raghunathan, "What motivates an attack on the homeless?," *Tampa Bay Times*, February 18, 2007.

88. The National Law Center on Homelessness & Poverty, "Homes Not Handcuffs: The Criminalization of Homelessness in U.S. Cities," (2009).

89. "This winter, new hope for homeless," *Tampa Bay Times*, November 15, 2007

90. "Pinellas Hope Fact Sheet," November 30, 2007, available at: http://unitedwaytampabay.files.wordpress.com/2007/12/pinellas-hope-fact-sheet-11-30-07.doc

91. "Tent City," St. Pete for Peace.

92. Baker, *Seamless City*, 180.

93. Ibid, 182.

94. Jimmy M., "Saw Your Blog..." E-mail message to author. April 20, 2012.

95. Anna M. Phillips, "County puts Pinellas Hope funding in budget permanently," *Tampa Bay Times*, September 15, 2012.

96. Pinellas County Health and Human Services, "Pinellas Hope: Reducing Street Homelessness," (2008).

97. David DeCamp, "Measuring Pinellas Hope project's success is proving difficult," *Tampa Bay Times*, May 9, 2009.

98. Peter Korn, "Handshake spurs deal to relocate R2DT camp," *Portland Tribune*, September 15, 2013.

99. Peter Korn, "Food carts gone; Chinatown lot owner fights back," *Portland Tribune*, June 22, 2011.

100. Mike B., Interview by author, October 22, 2011.

101. "Right 2 Dream Too," *Oregon Public Broadcasting*, October 19, 2011, radio interview available at: http://www.opb.org/radio/programs/thinkoutloud/segment/right-2-dream-too/

102. "Our History," Right 2 Dream Too website, available at: http://right-2dreamtoo.blogspot.com/p/our-history-past-and-present.html

103. Mark Hubbell, Interview by author, March 23, 2014.

104. Andrew Theen, "Right 2 Dream Too: Mayor Charlie Hales lauds homeless group, delays vote on move to Pearl District," *The Oregonian*, October 3, 2013.

105. Andrew Theen, "Right 2 Dream Too: Portland City Council approves $846,000 to help homeless community; Dan Saltzman walks out," *The Oregonian*, February 19, 2014.

106. Jack Tafari, "A brief history of the Out of the Doorways Campaign, part one," *Street Roots*, December 6, 2009.

107. Susan Finely, "The Faces of Dignity: Rethinking the politics of homelessness and poverty in America," *International Journal of Qualitative Studies in Education*, 16 (2003): 509.

108. Tracy J. Prince, "Portland's response to homeless issues and the broken windows theory," in *The Portland Edge: Challenges and successes in growing communities*, ed. Connie Ozawa (Washington: Island Press, 2004), 280-298.

109. "Dignity Village 2001 & Beyond: Outlining strategies for a sustainable future," June 2001, available at http://www.tentcitytoolkit.org

110. Ibid.

111. Finely, "Faces of Dignity."

112. The complete definition of ORS 446.265 can be found at: http://www.oregonlaws.org/ors/446.265

113. "Worksheet: Frequently-Asked Questions—An information sheet for neighbors," March 2007, available at http://www.tentcitytoolkit.org

114. Ibid

115. Ibid.

116. "Dignity Village 2001 & Beyond"

117. S. Verhovek, "In Oregon, A City Provides Public Land for the Homeless," *The New York Times*, September 10, 2001.

118. Kristina Smock Consulting, "An Evaluation of Dignity Village," 3 (2010).

119. Ray Kavick, "First week at Camp Quixote," *Works in Progress*, March 2007, full article available at: http://www.olywip.org/archive/page/article/2007/03/02.html

120. "CDBG Application—Program Year 2013" May 6, 2013.

121. "Public Hearing—Permanent Homeless Encampments," City Council Meeting, City of Olympia, WA, August 15, 2011.

122. Ibid.

123. "Findings, Conclusions and Decisions of the Hearing Examiner for the City of Olympia," City of Olympia, WA, April 30, 2012.

124. Ibid.

125. "Planning the Transformation from Camp Quixote to Quixote Village: A briefing paper about Panza and Camp Quixote's plan to turn a homeless tent community into a permanent Village," Panza, September 2010.

126. "CDBG Application."

127. Ibid.

128. "Opportunity Eugene: A Community Task Force on Homelessness Final Report and Recommendations," City of Eugene, OR, March 30, 2013.

129. "City Council Minutes – 12/10/12 Meeting," City of Eugene, OR, December 10, 2012.

130. Edward Russo, "Village Takes Root: Eugene's experiment in housing the homeless is achievign its goals," *The Register Gaurd*, June 15, 2014.

131. Edward Russo, "More Opportunity: Advocates plan to develop a new village for the homeless in Eugene," *The Register Gaurd*, May 30, 2014.

132. Jean Stacey, "2.9 js Life Boats and Sturdy Ships" E-mail message to author. February 10, 2014.

133. Paul Davidoff, "Advocacy and Pluralism in Planning," *Journal of the American Institute of Planners*, (November, 1965): 331-338.

Made in the USA
Middletown, DE
10 October 2015